HORIZON

MAY, 1960 · VOLUME II, NUMBER 5

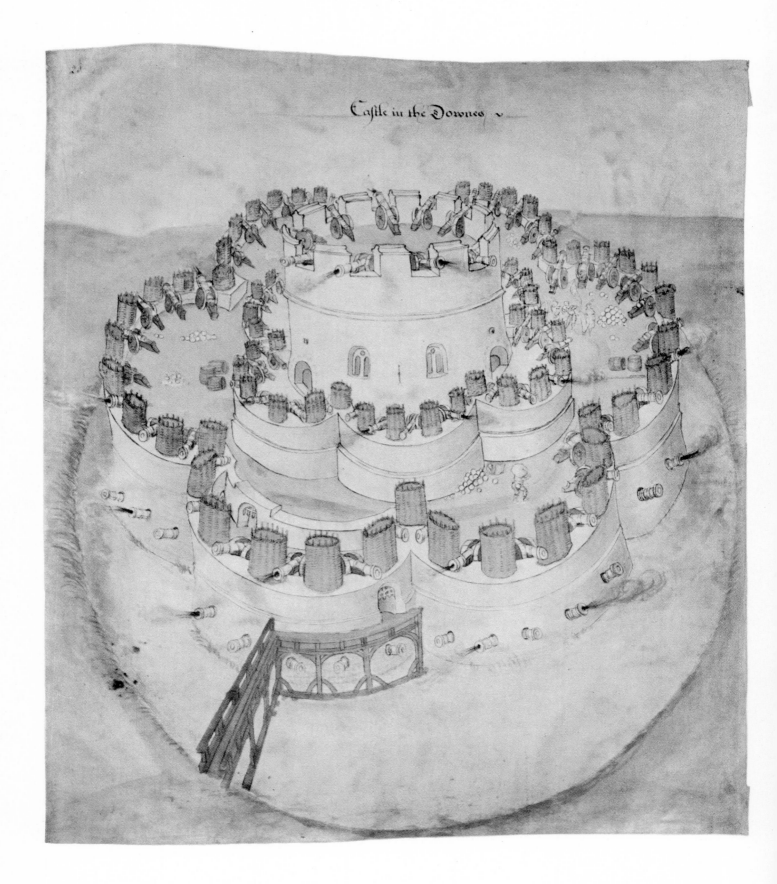

HORIZON

A Magazine of the Arts

MAY, 1960 · VOLUME II, NUMBER 5

PUBLISHER
James Parton

EDITOR
Joseph J. Thorndike, Jr.
MANAGING EDITOR
William Harlan Hale
ASSOCIATE EDITORS
Ralph Backlund
Robert Emmett Ginna
ASSISTANT EDITORS
Ada Pesin
Jane Wilson
CONTRIBUTING EDITOR
Margery Darrell
EDITORIAL ASSISTANTS
Shirley Abbott, Caroline Backlund,
Alan Doré, Martha Thomson

COPY EDITOR
Mary Ann Pfeiffer
Assistants: Rebecca R. Barocas, Ruth Limmer

ART DIRECTOR
Irwin Glusker
Assistant: Emma Landau

ADVISORY BOARD
Gilbert Highet, *Chairman*
Frederick Burkhardt   Oliver Jensen
Marshall B. Davidson   Jotham Johnson
Richard M. Ketchum

EUROPEAN CONSULTING EDITOR
J. H. Plumb
Christ's College, Cambridge

EUROPEAN BUREAU
Gertrudis Feliu, *Chief*
28 Quai du Louvre, Paris

CIRCULATION DIRECTOR
Richard V. Benson

HORIZON is published every two months by
American Horizon, Inc., a subsidiary of American
Heritage Publishing Co., Inc., 551 Fifth Avenue,
New York 17, N. Y.
      Single Copies: $3.95
Annual Subscriptions: $18.00 in the U.S. & Can.
                $19.00 elsewhere

Second-Class postage paid at New York, N.Y.

HORIZON welcomes contributions but can assume
no responsibility for such unsolicited material.

OUR FACE TO THE WORLD   *by Eric Larrabee*   4

THE HOUSATONIC   *Photographs by Hans Namuth*   10

A MEMORANDUM: FROM ELEANOR OF AQUITAINE
    TO ABIGAIL VAN BUREN AND ANN LANDERS   *by Morton M. Hunt* 30

THE CHILDHOOD PATTERN OF GENIUS   *by Harold G. McCurdy*   32

WHERE THE ROMANS ENJOYED "OMNIA COMMODA"
                                          by Lawrence Wright   39

THE SPECTRAL POETS OF PITTSBURGH   *by William Jay Smith*   42

THE NEW WAVE   *by Henry B. Darrach*   49

IN SEARCH OF THE ETRUSCANS   *by Raymond Bloch*   56

OUT OF A FAIR, A CITY   *by Ada Louise Huxtable*   80

A PASSION FOR IVORY   *by Ivan T. Sanderson*   88

THE RAMPANT FOX   *by Peter Quennell*   96

AN EASTERN ART GOES WESTERN   *by James A. Michener*   102

HOW TO MAKE THE ROUND TABLE SQUARE   *by Kenneth R. Morgan*   115

BETTER ENGLISH FOR THE 1960's?   119

FLORA'S FAUNA RISE IN REVOLT   *Drawings by Paul Flora*   120

THEIR NAMES ARE WRIT IN WEBSTER   *by Gilbert Highet*   126

THROUGH THE AGES IN THE BEST BEDS   129

COVER: This bearded visage, crowned with horns, is that of Achelous, great river god of the Greeks, as represented in an Etruscan pendant of the late sixth century B.C. The work, belonging to the Louvre, is testimony to Etruscan mastery of the goldsmith's art and to the fact that the Etruscans adopted this deity, like so many others, from the Greeks. The Etruscans and their arts are the subject of an article beginning on page 56.

FRONTISPIECE: Billowing like a decorated mushroom, the "Castle in the Downse" at Sandown, Kent, might at this very moment be training its cannon on invading French ships in the English Channel. In 1545, France sent an armada to retaliate against England's invasion of Boulogne the previous year. Henry VIII built a series of these purely defensive castles on the southern coast in the 1540's, thereby changing the character of the castle from an impregnable residence of the independent noble to one built by central royal authority for national defense. This water color is in the British Museum.

THE RELUCTANT AMBASSADORS

The GIs of World War II, wanting only to have done with it and come home, conveyed more of their country's character than they knew. In the late Robert Capa's photograph, a paratrooper of the 82nd Airborne Division, at the capture of Palermo, is surrounded and reached out to as an object of wonderment by Sicilian children.

Our Face to the World

As the grudging inheritor of imperial power, America

exports huge cultural influence even despite itself,

and now sees its image reflected around the globe

By ERIC LARRABEE

Sometime during this year, if conditions are favorable, the following events will take place. A book will be published containing a collection of essays about America by foreign observers. At least one United States Embassy abroad will be stoned by an angry mob. A communist government will denounce the addiction of its youth to decadent Western habits, such as the hula-hoop. A congressman will call for the cessation of foreign aid. Our own government will be attacked by a European intellectual for "murdering" the Rosenbergs, using biological warfare in Korea, and corrupting European culture through the introduction of absinthe-flavored drinking straws. Either Arnold J. Toynbee or Barbara Ward will reply, in a magazine article asserting that the fundamental challenge of the twentieth century can be met only by the Americans, and that it remains to be seen whether or not they are equal to that mighty task.

The details may be different, but the essentials of the annual routine are now fixed, a set of conventions as rigid as those requiring taxi drivers to be philosophical, or presidential candidates to wear funny hats. The world has become accustomed to worrying about us, and we have become accustomed to seeing ourselves in the mirror of its reactions. Indeed, we originated in an act of self-consciousness about what other people would think—being moved, so we said, by "a decent respect to the opinions of mankind"—and we have not quite lost this innocent sense of being on trial before the bar of history.

Traditionally, we use foreign visitors as an excuse for self-analysis. The arrival of Mr. Khrushchev last year was an opportunity for anyone who so desired to single out what was typical or important for him to see, and it was widely seized, among others by President Eisenhower, who gave his own listing in a press conference: Levittown, "our great industrial plants," some middle western farmland, "the little town where I was reared," an air view of Washington, "a happy people . . . doing exactly as they choose." Selections like these amount to a definition of one's country, an image of what it might be if not what it is; and best of all, for a professedly extrovert people, they offer a chance to be introspective without admitting it.

Through the voices of critical travelers we can also hear, and then virtuously deny, our own suspicions about ourselves. We ask itinerant foreigners to tell us the worst, on the assumed grounds that we do not wish to tell it to each other. All down the years—from Mrs. Trollope to Simone de Beauvoir—surely the dissatisfied diarists were rare who failed to find an American audience for the record of their voyages. We faithfully remember their epigrams—among the best is Oscar Wilde's, to the effect that Niagara Falls would be more impressive if the water ran in the other direction—and Sydney Smith earned himself immortality in America by asking who, in the four corners of the world, ever read an American book?

Few have understood this national masochism better than George Bernard Shaw. "To rouse their eager interest," he wrote, "their distinguished consideration and their undying devotion, all that is necessary is to hold them up to the ridicule of the rest of the universe. Dickens won them to him forever by merciless projections of typical Americans as windbags, swindlers and assassins . . . I myself have been particularly careful never to say a civil word to the United States. I have scoffed at their inhabitants as a nation of villagers. I have defined the 100 per cent American as 99 per cent idiot. And they just adore me."

By the same token, when a non-native has something good to say for us, his words are doubly valued. Presumably he knows all our sins, and grants the virtues only after the severest examination. As a result, if there is a single classic book *about* America, it is de Tocqueville's; and the least of his most restrained and hesitant characterizations of us has an authority here comparable to that of Holy Writ. His only rival today is another European, Denis Brogan, and the list is long of current books in praise of America written either by non-Americans—like Wyndham Lewis, Luigi Barzini, and Father Bruckberger—or by acclimatized Americans like Alistair Cooke, Peter Drucker, and Jacques Barzun.

In the view of a stranger, one's own country takes on freshness and abstraction. He does not see it, as we do, in terms of the dreary and familiar, or measure its achievement by a picayune scorekeeping of daily gains and pains. Everything comes at him on a flood tide of brand-new sense impressions, all of a piece; and they all must be significant, because each incident *is* America. He sees not the specific fact, with its annoying complexity and indefiniteness, but the idea, the generality that might help him cope with so much strangeness. The gritty surface of society is no less visible to him. He is just as likely to notice the dirt and ugliness that still play so large a part in American physical and psychic life. But they come to him lifted above the particular to a level of the safe and the significant.

In recent years we have acquired further incentives to visualize ourselves in terms of a foreign audience from the desire, first, to win the postwar propaganda contest with the Soviet Union and, second, to package and export the "American way" (whatever that should be) to the underdeveloped areas of Asia and Africa. The two causes have sometimes had a tendency to intermingle, with disastrous effects, since the charms of the opulent "American way" are not always appealing to the less fortunate, and since it is difficult enough to revolutionize other societies without asking them to love us in the process. The outcome, in any event, is increased pressure on Americans to project themselves against a world-wide backdrop and to judge the merits of their own performance on an international stage. There is noisy public discussion as to whether our exhibit at the Moscow Fair was representative and effective; and in popular novels about the tropics or the Far East, there is now a new breed of stock characters, the Americans—nice Americans, quiet Americans, ugly Americans—who come out into the former colonial empires with naïve idealism in their hearts and bright, altruistic platitudes on their lips.

These Americans—engineers and agronomists, doctors and economists, scholars and administrators—have been abroad in large numbers only during the past decade, but they already occupy a powerful symbolic position. They speak for an America that is pleasant to contemplate, a country eager to give away not so much the products of its abundance as the secret of how abundance is achieved—not to help others, out of mere charity, but to help others help themselves. This is the America that backed Point IV and the U.N. Technical Assistance programs, a nation linked to its missionary past and its national self-interest in a future where the gap be-

INSIDIOUS PROPAGANDA FROM THE DECADENT WEST

The products of our popular culture often prove more irresistible abroad than our foreign policy. The hula-hoop was everywhere: Italy (left), Africa (center), and Japan (right).

*THE JAPANESE ROYAL
FAMILY TURNS INFORMAL*

*In Japan, even royalty proved susceptible to Western influence. At left,
Hirohito with a tieless MacArthur, 1945; right, Akihito and bride, 1959.*

tween rich lands and poor will be less abysmal. Historically we share this mission with Western Europe, and it is the "main issue"—as C. P. Snow called it in his Rede Lectures in 1959—of the scientific revolution of our era.

This country, with the undoubted distinction of being the most *over*developed nation in the world, is the one others have naturally turned to as an example of advanced industrialism. They have often turned to it, however, in a divided state of mind. They would like to adopt our technology without adopting our social philosophy. They are tempted to believe, as C. P. Snow himself seems sometimes to believe, that technology is simply a neutral instrument. Snow writes as a scientist and a European, preoccupied with the division in Western culture between the sciences and the humanities, and thus he offers little argument against those who think technology capable of being applied in any society, under any moral or ethical system whatever. There are many such who would like to have steel mills without having juke boxes, to have highways and hospitals without having all the vulgarity and disorder that goes with "a happy people," as President Eisenhower put it, "doing exactly as they choose."

Now if there is anything the Americans know—if there is any one lesson they can abstract from their experience and leave behind them—it is that this divorce, between industrial technique and the society that uses it, will not work. The same machines are not equally productive in different countries, nor does the productivity of American machines result from any innate superiority. The many European experts who came here after the war to inspect them often reported that our machines were inferior to theirs; our ad-

vantage was in the attitude of the men and women who ran them. Mass production works only when there is a mass market to support it, and the importation of American mass marketing—under whatever ideology—will bring other aspects of mass culture with it. Western Europe has since been drastically increasing its own productivity, and a by-product has been the timid emergence of lower-middle-class consumers' taste that goes there under the name of "Americanization." Of course, that is a misnomer, for it is no more than what must always happen when you industrialize effectively.

Henry James said that the American way is more different from other national ways than they are from one another; and, if this were true, it would not be surprising if our characteristic products, from the highest to the lowest, had much in common. "From pragmatism to the movies," writes Bertrand Russell, "is not such a far cry as might be thought." Again, it has been the outsiders who have appreciated that the parts of this culture fit together, and cannot be exported selectively. "The impact of America on the outside world . . ." as Denis Brogan once said, "is far more revolutionary than most Americans think, because we think of it as the arrival of Cadillacs or Coca-Cola or anything else, without realizing that in the same ship—so to speak, in the same package— they are bringing a whole series of ideas, habits, and concepts, which must all hang together. Otherwise you won't have industrialization. . . ."

Lacking this awareness that they are revolutionaries, some Americans may suffer from the delusion that their country's impact on others is weak. Indeed, at the very moment when the rest of the world has been scared stiff of

"Americanization," we have been sitting at home lamenting our failure to "sell ourselves" more effectively. From the foreigners' point of view, any American object or idea represents a profoundly unsettling and unpredictable threat. Our most ordinary products, by their manufacturers' deliberate plan, carry the built-in capacity to stimulate aspiration, to suggest that life need not always be the same; and they may strike through to the public anywhere, totally without warning, as happened in Jakarta in 1955, when an American model toy train completely captivated the Indonesian crowds at a trade fair and drew them away from a building five times as large, in which the Communist Chinese were exhibiting machine tools, lathes, and dynamos.

What seems like a guileless and unaggressive position from our point of view, may look from someone else's—as it was described by the president of the East Berlin Academy of Arts—like a "militant, crusading ideology." American popular culture has an unequaled penetrating power, for it is a response to exactly that pent-up appetite for better things that industrialism is now releasing elsewhere. We tend not to think of ourselves as responsible for the spread of soft drinks or rock-'n'-roll records, or what can only be called the "American style" in juvenile delinquency—the Teddy Boys in England or the *stilyagi* in Russia—yet the custodians of Things as They Always Were, in whatever country, can only regard these phenomena as manifestations of a single spreading poison, an irresistible tide of nastiness that America has set in motion.

Of course, we are not wholly surprised to be disliked for such things, since we dislike them ourselves, and we have almost got over the desire to be universally beloved. But we are still a little dismayed to be hated for something we didn't know we were doing, or were doing only absent-mindedly—that is, reorganizing the world in our image. Our very dismay is itself an additional reason for people to distrust us. Anti-Americanism takes many forms, most of them relatively unimportant, but the most intense and long-lasting antipathies we attract come from the fear that the Americans do not know what they are up to, that they are good people tinkering with forces they can neither understand nor control, children playing with the Promethean fire.

The American villains who now turn up in novels—as in Graham Greene's *The Quiet American*—are essentially cast in this mold, parodies of what we would like to think of as our virtues. Freedom from caste snobbery, belief in human perfectibility, pursuit of power over nature, dedication to alleviating mankind's suffering—given sufficient skill or malice, these are now all blended into fictional characters who are clumsy, amoral, doomed, and, above all, dangerously ignorant. Modern readers, even American readers, can apparently accept as credible a "typical" American who is idealistic only because he can afford to be, democratic only because he has no cultural roots, scientific only because he is arrogant, and optimistic only because he knows no better.

Numerous European writers still compare us to the Romans, since the normal tactic of any civilization, compelled to hand on the torch to another, is to imply that its successor is brutish and administrative. But it was a Swiss journalist writing under the name of Robert Jungk, a shrewd and pertinacious observer of the United States, who gave the most extreme description of how presumptuous our posture may appear. In his book *Tomorrow Is Already Here,* Jungk declared that the Americans were "fundamentally more ambitious than even their sharpest adversaries believe. Their efforts do not aspire to the mastery of continents, still less to the entire globe, but to higher things far than these. America is striving to win power over the sum total of things, complete and absolute mastery of nature in all its aspects. . . . The stake is higher than dictators' seats and presidential chairs. The stake is the throne of God."

Even discounting the excess of language, or the enthusiasm of a writer letting a metaphor run away with him, there is no escaping such an indictment except by pleading incompetence. The Russians have since come along to save us from any more such accusations, and now we can at least claim to be fallible, even as other heaven-storming peoples before us; but what is mainly wrong with Mr. Jungk's statement is its obsolescence and exclusiveness. Among his Americans, loaded to the teeth with *hubris*, I fail to recognize so many of my fellow countrymen—Foreign Service officers, foundation executives, army officers, academics, bankers, overseas journalists, or miscellaneous amateurs—who are presently concerned with wondering what their country stands for. They are, if anything, the opposite of falsely proud: they are overburdened with reflectiveness, sensitive to the limitations on action, modest in their objectives, sophisticated in method, and soft in speech to the point of near-inaudibility.

The demand for Americans to represent us to the world has indeed brought forward a new type—or, rather, made prominent an old one. He is, if you like, a missionary of the secular cult of Americanization. He is the mild expert, the seasoned campaigner in public service, the embodiment of our best habits of civic responsibility. His virtues come from his competence; his vices, from his obligation to act out the role of a superior being, however uncomfortable it makes him. Somewhere at his inner core must be some residue of national assertiveness, but it need not be the arrogance that Jungk describes—nor does his arrogance mark him. What marks him is worry.

In the ten or so years that we have been trying to take over the running of the globe from the exhausted Europeans, we have almost managed to equal them in a sad and worldly awareness of the multiple prices of power. One by one, our former swords of righteousness have turned in our hands and cut us, so that generals have become our most persuasive pacifists and organizations that used to send out medical teams to save lives are now anxious about overpopulation.

When foreign students and scholars now attend conferences to talk about the future, it is they who are likely to be fired by the ancient faith—who demand hygiene, tractors, and the other blessings—while it is the Americans who draw back and say: Gently, gently, not so fast; it is not all that simple.

True, the task of dealing with far continents and strange tongues does not yet command the best American talents. Life within the continental boundaries is still far too fascinating to most of us to provide the necessary surplus of unused, first-class energies. Many of our compatriots whom Asians and Africans first encounter belong to what I have heard called, without kindness, the Friends of the Underdeveloped Areas—a class of unemployables left over from the 1930's and progressive schools, whose zeal for humanity in the abstract is matched only by their distaste for it in the particular. And creeping after them have come their enemies from the far-out Right, still looking for a deep-laid plot to subvert the Republic by sending milk to Hottentots.

Yet it is also true that the mission of carrying the "American" message to the corners of a waiting planet attracts many who, for thoroughly decent reasons, are out of step with their fellows. Perhaps they believe in all-out effort, in testing themselves, or in activity for its own sake. Perhaps they are dissatisfied with a homeland that seems to have gone soft, that no longer has any goal worth striving for, or that resolves its problems by postponement. "As Americans begin to rise above the industrial evangelism of our own past," David Riesman remarks, "we make things very uncomfortable for those of us who are too much in love with the older definitions of efficiency. [Those] now in demand [are the] men who don't drive too hard, men who can create a happy atmosphere among companionable work groups, men who aren't too infuriated with waste. Sometimes I think we tend to export our remaining zealots of efficiency, on Point IV or Ford Foundation missions, where they can speak for 'American methods' as they never could at home."

C. P. Snow talked about the "main issue" of economic development as though it posed forbidding obstacles and was therefore worth the attention of serious people. Something of this challenge in "development" has already attracted many alert and thoughtful intelligences; and in our brief experiment with it we have already accumulated a fund of what Harlan Cleveland, dean of the Maxwell School at Syracuse, calls by the awkward name of "overseasmanship"—the capacity to surmount the innumerable practical difficulties of putting good will to work in unpromising circumstances. But dedication and competence (or even money, which Snow and others emphasize) will not be enough if we project only a fragmentary image of America, if we fail to convey the essential elements of our experience. Here, as in the other confrontations between our country and the world, the same old questions are posed again: What kind of impression are we trying to make? What kind of people are we?

Not a few Americans—George F. Kennan and Walter Lippmann being the most notable—would like to see our idealistic, missionary stance abandoned and replaced with the cool calculation of national self-interest. Some who have administered aid programs abroad have been known to return with the conviction that American altruism is an unworkable basis for policy. One official I interviewed in Washington once went so far as to argue that since no European in his right mind believes that America wishes only to "help" other countries, we should concoct some venal and devious motives—if necessary, out of whole cloth—which other people could at least accept as credible.

And why, now that you mention it, should we want everyone else to be like us? We are none too pleased with our own traditional characteristics. The bustling busyness that

CONTINUED ON PAGE 122

A NATIVE DANCE, FOR THE NATIVES

Barriers between cultures are broken down by natural spontaneity. The smiling Pacific Islanders in the front row of this audience in New Britain in 1944 had just finished demonstrating their own songs and dances when these American Marines responded in kind. Something of the national character is shown in the fact that their names were duly reported home: John N. Giordani and Rocco Mitchell, both of Massachusetts.

Where nature and tradition meet: the covered bridge across the Housatonic at West Cornwall

A lean New England river

carved a valley

that has become a haven

for creative spirits from

Hawthorne's time to Thurber's.

Here man and nature

still collaborate.

Its leading inhabitants today

compose a brilliant gallery of talents

THE
HOUSATONIC

What distinguishes the Housatonic is that it is less a waterway than a retreat; it encourages not so much commerce as a state of mind. Rising in the Berkshires, it descends lean and linear over four falls and 115 miles of rolling western New England into Long Island Sound. As American rivers go, it is neither grand nor dashing; when compared to the scale of the mighty Mississippi, the Missouri, the Columbia, or the neighboring Hudson, it hardly rates as more than one of our better creeks. If sheer charm of scenery is the test, the mountainous Juniata is more sinuous, the Wabash more soft and mild. Still, over the years, men and women busied in the arts have singled out the Housatonic's valley as a refuge in numbers out of all proportion to its size. They have done so partly because it is so accessible, partly because it has proved itself so impractical, and perhaps also—consciously or not—because it is so independent. For, small as it is, the Housatonic is no other river's tributary. It strikes on its own from freshets to the sea.

The river's impracticality appeared early, in the falls and rapids that hampered Connecticut's seaboard settlers in their urge to tap, exploit, and then mechanize its watershed. Yet the Valley lay near enough to the centers of Hartford and New Haven to obtain the ministrations of their divines. So it received the spirit but little of the sustenance of Puritanism; and it was this emphasis on mind as against matter that

helped this most neglected New England river eventually become—paradoxically or not—its most cosmopolitan one.

Soon thoughtful and restless men as far away as Boston and New York discovered it to be accessible to them, too, as a peaceable haven. The year 1850, when the Merrimac, the Connecticut, and the Hudson were already buzzing with mills along their lower reaches, saw three major American men of letters converge upon the upper Housatonic for its simplicity and silence: Nathaniel Hawthorne of Salem, to write *The House of the Seven Gables*, Herman Melville of Manhattan and the sea, to write *Moby Dick*, and their urbane friend Oliver Wendell Holmes of Beacon Street, to regale them both on occasion with good talk and champagne.

If it was a sort of dreamland then, much of the Valley remains an enclave now—a narrow wooded wedge thrust from the north almost within sight of Connecticut's chimneys and almost (but not quite) within commuting range of New York. The split-levels and the stations lined with sports cars cease well below New Milford. Beyond, we have what some call escape and others an odd geographical accident.

Short as it seems, the Valley is too long and rangy to form a unity or anything like a cultural "colony." There have been and there are a few nuclei along the way, but the river that so retarded commerce also does not encourage Togetherness. There was the parasoled, white-flannel-trouser era of the great summer mansions around Stockbridge, with Edith Wharton and the renowned lawyer-diplomat Joseph H. Choate its presiding deities and Henry James often up for weekends. There is Tanglewood. There are such lesser community attempts as Yelping Hill at Cornwall. But mostly there is quiet and apartness.

These pages present a gallery of distinguished Valley citizens whose homes or work places range from headwaters to estuary. Mostly they live in clapboard houses set far apart along the slopes, and while there is at times concerted music and always a great clacking of individual typewriters, the characteristic sounds of the Valley still remain the scuffle of woodland rodents, the purling of small waters over granite, and the sputtering of a remote tractor out to cultivate a lean field.

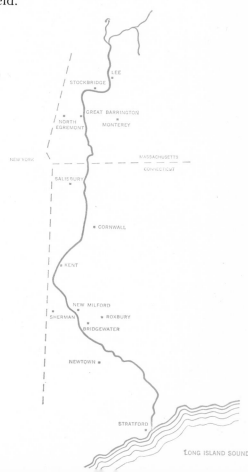

NORMAN ROCKWELL (left) is doubtless the best known among a number of famous persons who live in Stockbridge, Massachusetts, a historic town through which the Housatonic flows, twenty miles south of one of its sources, Pontoosuc Lake. Although he moved there from Vermont only in 1953, by now Rockwell seems to have posed every second Stockbridge citizen for his canvases. The more than three hundred covers he has created for the *Saturday Evening Post* and his World War II paintings of the Four Freedoms have made him America's most prominent illustrator. He lives in a big white house on U.S. route 7, which follows the Housatonic, and works in a red barn-studio a few steps away. Ardent in his pursuit of perfection (many years ago he lettered the symbol "100%" at the top of his easel), Rockwell has vied with the most exuberant abstract expressionist for effects; once he rubbed a *Post* cover-canvas full of garden dirt to get the tone and texture he wanted.

PHOTOGRAPHED FOR HORIZON BY HANS NAMUTH

TED SHAWN (left) has made his cluster of handsome weathered buildings at Jacob's Pillow, near Lee, Massachusetts, one of America's cultural landmarks. There in 1942 he erected the first theater in the United States designed for the dance. Since then, the Jacob's Pillow Dance Festival has attracted growing audiences and has drawn youths from all over the world who come to study every aspect of dance with Shawn and his faculty. Co-founder with his wife, Ruth St. Denis, of the pioneering Denishawn Dancers and, later, founder of a unique, all-male company, Shawn is also an impresario and author as well as a master mason, constantly adding stonework to his growing establishment. Amid his intense outpouring of energy at sixty-nine, he likes to relax by sitting on the boulder that gives the place its name, looking out over the upper reaches of the Housatonic Valley.

"THE INDEPENDENT SIX" is the collective name assumed by the painters and sculptors seated below, all residents of the Berkshires in the general neighborhood of Monterey, Massachusetts, where this photograph was taken. Two years ago they joined to form a co-operative for mutual advancement, sometimes traveling and exhibiting together. The members are (from the left, each with a recent representative work in the background): Roy Lindstrom and his "Roadside Barn," Fred Lancome and "Hindu Rhythm," Stanley Bate and "Resting Warrior," Homer Gunn and "Wind," Franc Epping and "The Musician," Harry Lane and "Façade." No common school or style unites "The Independent Six," who regard their venture as "an experiment in diversity and artistic tolerance." Their alliance is formed on friendship and a common devotion to the Housatonic and the Berkshires.

MAC MORGAN (right) lives in Stockbridge in a spacious house whose garden, partly shown here, was designed by the late Daniel Chester French, the sculptor. A young baritone of exceptional versatility, Morgan has been acclaimed in recitals, as soloist with America's leading orchestras, and—during the past two seasons, for example—in such varied works as Igor Stravinsky's *Threni*, Berlioz's *L'Enfance du Christ*, and Mozart's *Così fan Tutte* (with the NBC Opera Company). He is a far better actor than most operatic performers and, for a number of years, has played straight dramatic roles in summer stock near his home. As a boy in Jacksonville, Florida, his enthusiasms were tennis and the trombone. A faculty member at the New England Conservatory of Music in Boston, Morgan is married to a pianist, Helen Neilly; they have three daughters, all of whom sing.

RICHARD DYER-BENNET (left), tenor and guitarist, is today's counterpart of the medieval troubadour. With a repertory of six hundred songs, from folk ballads to Beethoven, he tours the concert halls of America and Europe, re-creating the works of ancient bards with extraordinary purity of voice, elegance of accompaniment, and evocation of mood. His performances—and the fact that he is listed in *Burke's Peerage* as the cousin of a baronet—make it seem surprising that, while a student at the University of California, he considered returning to his native England as a professional soccer player. Instead, he visited an aging Swedish minstrel, Sven Scholander, and came away determined to spend his life singing. With his wife, two daughters, and a Weimaraner, Dyer-Bennet lives deep in the Berkshire woods near Great Barrington in a modern house, where he tapes his recordings.

ZINO FRANCESCATTI (right) spends his winters on the concert stages of the world, resting between engagements at his French home near the city of his birth, Marseilles. But for his summers as well as some winter weekends, he retires to his mountaintop estate, Fiddletop, overlooking the Housatonic watershed near Monterey. There he prepares his programs and entertains old friends who share a love of conversation with the volatile Marseillais. Originally educated for the law at the wish of a tempestuous Italian father who was himself a violinist, he received his musical education initially from his mother—also a violinist—and then married a violinist who sat behind him in the Poulet Orchestra of Paris. Hailed as "the prince of virtuosi" in his youth, he has since won lasting rank among those masters for whom the heart is no less important than the head and hands.

ROBERT OSBORN has lived in Salisbury, Connecticut, in the shadow of the Taconic range of the Berkshires, since 1946, when he began the free-lance career that has made him one of America's best-known
cartoonists. Here he is seen outside his studio beside a sculpture given him by Alexander Calder (who
lives in nearby Roxbury) and his own painting "Skeleton as a Matador." First a painter, Osborn began
full-time cartooning during World War II, when his safety posters for Navy flyers won him the Legion
of Merit. Among later tributes to his turbulent, incisive drawings in magazines and books (*The
Exurbanites, Parkinson's Law, Osborn on Leisure*), he is proudest of his colleague Herblock's remark.
"You've done for cartooning what Freud did for psychology." Osborn himself says his work tries to
express "the steady plight of man, the anarchy of his laughter, the terrifying lawlessness of his tragedies."

RUSSELL LYNES is rare among "summer people" in that he has lived in the Berkshires, in the upper reaches of the Housatonic Valley, longer than many of the "natives." He was, in fact, born in Great Barrington, where his father was Episcopal rector, and this red barn—to which he sometimes retires to do some writing—is only a few score feet from the house in North Egremont which his family has owned since 1927. Lynes has been variously a ship's scullion, a fire-extinguisher salesman, a training specialist in the Pentagon, and principal—with his wife—of a girls' school. Now managing editor of *Harper's*, he is master of the social commentary on both past and present that earned him *The New Yorker's* accolade: "one of our truly dead-eye generalizers." Among the books to reinforce this judgment are *The Tastemakers* (1954), *A Surfeit of Honey* (1957), and *Cadwallader: A Diversion* (1959).

JAMES THURBER (right) lives in Cornwall, Connecticut, in a 90-year-old house once owned by the man who invented the honeycomb automobile radiator. All Thurber invents is some of the smoothest and funniest prose being written in English today. He has been doing this for years, in places as far-flung as the *New Yorker* office, Bermuda, England, Hollywood, and now the Housatonic Valley. The locale is not important: "I can write upside down in a boiler room." When failing sight forced him to give up the typewriter in 1941, he began using pencils and yellow copy paper—twenty words to a sheet, a hundred words to a pencil. Now he writes mainly in his head. Because he usually has twelve to fifteen pieces simmering there at once, he is reluctant to be interrupted by interviewers or photographers. "We have photographers," he says, "the way other households have mice."

LEWIS GANNETT (left) was an editor of *The Nation* when, in 1924, he bought as a weekend retreat an old farmhouse on Cream Hill above the village of West Cornwall and its covered bridge, unaware when he did so that his great-great-grandfather, President Ezra Stiles of Yale, had farmed some acres close to his own five generations before. Little had changed along the back roads between them in all the intervening time. While winning prominence as the book critic of the New York *Herald Tribune*, Gannett also became a devoted countryman, as expert in the lore of ferns, wildflowers, and garden produce as in that of the modern novel and the latest twist of sociology. World traveler, war correspondent, authority on many byways of American history, his interests have ranged far, but nothing so commands his energy as bringing in crops to swell his cellars as books do his rooms.

MARK VAN DOREN (right) with his late brother Carl and their wives Dorothy and Irita established the Housatonic Valley's nearest approach to a literary colony when they settled in Cornwall in the 1920's—their colony consisting entirely of Van Dorens. Carl, the elder, arrived first, having preceded Mark from the Illinois prairies to Columbia University and into a brilliant writing and teaching career. Much of the younger brother's writing has been done in summer or sabbatical months in a bare cubicle in an old sawmill beside a pond at the end of a meadow. Now retired from teaching, he has year-round time to roam the 150 acres that are his spiritual home, tinker in his shop, and continue that flow of poems, novels, stories, and critical studies that have made a leading man of letters of the spare Middle Westerner whose first book, significantly, was a study of Thoreau.

MALCOLM COWLEY (left), critic, poet, and editor, poses with a small sampling of the printed matter which each year inundates his Sherman home. A resident of the Housatonic Valley since 1926, Cowley was one of the early intellectuals to discover its singular attractions: pleasant scenery, low property taxes (today no longer the case), and proximity to New York. When not writing, he can usually be found with one of his two garden tractors—the metamorphosis from literary country squire to man with a mechanical hoe is complete. His special pride and constant retreat is the acre of pine woods behind his house; pruned and manicured, it looks like a German forest in miniature. Much of his free time, however, is spent warring with the woodchucks. In his upstairs bathroom he keeps a .22 rifle; and from this vantage point, many a trespassing rodent has met its end.

LÉONIE ADAMS (right) and her husband, the critic William Troy, bought their house on the top of Candlewood Mountain, west of New Milford, back in 1934. There she writes the kind of poems that prompted Allen Tate to say: "More than anyone else today she continues at the highest level the great lyrical tradition of the English Romantics, with whom in their own time she would have held her own." Miss Adams, in *her* own time, has held her own to the extent of winning most of the major poetry awards—last November it was the $5000 Fellowship Award of the Academy of American Poets—and of being appointed the Consultant in Poetry at the Library of Congress for 1948–49. Born in Brooklyn, the unlikely nursery of so many poets, she has never celebrated it in verse. Rather, she writes of woods, wind, the changing seasons, and the moody climate of the heart.

EDMUND FULLER (left) teaches English at Kent School, on the west bank of the Housatonic, and writes novels and criticism in a hillside house a short distance upstream, where he lives with his wife and four children. His beard gives him the look of an unusually well-barbered prophet—a role he does not claim for himself but that one feels he would not find uncongenial. In his most recent (and most considerable) work of criticism, *Man in Modern Fiction*, he declares that "only a minority among those calling themselves, formally, Christians or Jews, have a profound and actively conscious awareness of what it is that these great religions actually teach about our nature as man. This is a major reason for the diminishing vision our recent age has had of our kind." That "diminishing vision" he attacks in contemporary writing—but with wit, urbanity, and surprising good temper.

RUSSELL COWLES, the well-known artist, is an Iowan by birth, and a member of a family famous in the newspaper world. Though his brothers Gardner and John both became publishers (of *Look* and the Minneapolis *Star* and *Tribune*, respectively), Russell Cowles rejected journalism for painting. For more than twenty years he has made his home in New Milford, Connecticut. He and his wife, the writer Nancy Cardozo, live in a century-old stone house (seen in the background) surrounded by the great maples which are so much a part of the Housatonic scene. Somewhat remote even in this age of sprawling developments, his house is set off on one of the few unpaved roads remaining in the area. For Cowles, the abundance of nature in these surroundings provides constant subject matter for his paintings; he finds the almost pastoral setting of the Housatonic Valley an ideal place in which to work as well as live.

PETER BLUME is an artist whose sweeping allegories are as carefully painted and accurately detailed as miniatures. In comparison to most contemporary painters, his output is small; he has spent an average of three years on each of his major works. Born in Russia and raised in Brooklyn, he moved to Sherman. Connecticut, in 1930. His curious but charming house is a remodeled barn; high and narrow, it looks from the outside like an over-sized bird feeding station. Such a comparison is not altogether inappropriate, for Blume and his wife are both amateur ornithologists. Few visitors are as welcome as a redbird or a rare flock of evening grosbeaks, and the Blumes share the attentions of a tame chickadee named "McGinnit" with their neighbor across the road. Malcolm Cowley. In this photograph, Blume poses with a recent painting at the edge of a newly dug pond which he has named "Lake Ebie" after his wife.

VAN WYCK BROOKS knows the character of New England and the great figures of its past as well as he knows the clapboards of this Congregational church directly across the way from his house in Bridgewater, Connecticut. He was already famed for a long shelf of critical and historical studies, ranging from *The Ordeal of Mark Twain* to *The Flowering of New England,* when in 1949 he moved to this quiet village to continue his re-evaluation of American literature. There he lives with his wife, the writer Gladys Rice Billings, in a gray McKinley-era mansion that dominates the countryside from behind its white railing. Stick in hand, he regularly sets forth to walk the country roads, noting the way a different growth of grass marks an old Indian footpath or the way sunlight falls on farmhouse windowpanes. At home, he works in a room toppling with books old and new and hung with photographs of men whom he knows like table companions: Whitman, Melville, Howells. Young writers seek him out for his knowledge and spirit, and find a hospitable latchstring.

WILLIAM STYRON (left), one of the most talented of our younger novelists, is a comparative newcomer to the Housatonic. A Virginian by birth, who wrote of his native state in a notable first novel, *Lie Down in Darkness,* Styron lived in New York and Europe before moving with his wife to a clapboard farmhouse in Roxbury, Connecticut, in 1954. Explaining why he chose to live there, Styron says, "A young writer probably needs the contact of other people like himself and the rub of a big city like New York or Paris. But there comes a time when you have had that. I have." By habit a night owl, Styron has of late taken up astronomy in a modest way. He complains, however, that the New England atmosphere is not always conducive to star gazing. His third novel, *Set This House on Fire,* begun on a Fellowship in Literature to the American Academy in Rome, will be published in June.

LAWRENCE LANGNER (right), although he himself lives in Cannondale, Connecticut, some distance from the lower Housatonic, belongs to the Valley by virtue of his leading role in the founding and building of the American Shakespeare Festival Theater at Stratford, at the river's mouth. Here he is seen on the playhouse balcony. Langner's vision, too, has led to the creation of the permanent American Shakespeare Academy to train actors for productions of the master playwright's works. His plans call also for the erection of a Shakespeare Museum for this sixth summer of the Festival. A Welshman by birth, Langner has been an international patent lawyer for forty-seven years, finding time also to conceive and direct the Theatre Guild, father the Westport Country Playhouse, and write a number of successful books and plays, several with his wife, Armina Marshall.

LOUIS UNTERMEYER (left) is best known as an anthologist of other people's poetry; but he is also a distinguished poet in his own right—a man who has written, edited, or translated some seventy-one books during a long career. His private life reflects his varied interests and enthusiasms. A native New Yorker, Untermeyer set out to be a pianist, gave up music to go into his family's jewelry business—which, in turn, he left to devote himself to writing. He has raised cats, flowers, sugar maples, cows, and Eskimo dogs. In this photograph, he sits in his flower garden (Untermeyer could probably anthologize botany almost as well as poetry), displaying in his lap a framed embroidery of a cat. Cats are a passion—he keeps five of them—as are puns and the color blue. He wears blue, lives in a blue colonial cottage in Newtown, Connecticut, and even writes in a blue barn.

A MEMORANDUM

From: Eleanor of Aquitaine

To: Abigail van Buren and Ann Landers

Subject: The Present Condition of Love-Counselling

Ye worthy dames and notable scriveners, Eleanor, Duchess of Aquitaine, whilom Queen of France, and thereafter Queen of England, sends you greeting.

Impelled by a sense of duty, we reluctantly proffer you some unsolicited criticisms. For it seems to us that both the theory and the practice of love-counselling, as exemplified in your pre-eminent selves, have fallen lamentably far from the standards we established in the years 1170 to 1173, when we now and again convened the Court of Love in our palace at Poitiers and, together with other noble ladies, interpreted the code of *courtesie* in divers cases that came before us.

To begin with, dear twin sisters of each other, the competition between your syndicated columns, "Dear Abby" and "Ann Landers Says," has caused you to indulge in a celebrated public feud, in which you openly belittle and denigrate each other. This we find altogether unseemly in you; the spokeswomen of Love ought always to display *gravitas* and a divine sweetness. Poets and courtiers worshipped ourself for our beauty, dignity, and refinement; wherefore our name is still found in your bookstores seven and a half centuries after we left your earthly domain. The vulgar commotions in which you accuse each other of pilfering ideas, cutting syndicate rates, and the like, have gotten you writ upon the pages of *Time* and *Life*, which is little more than to be writ upon water. Who speaks on behalf of Love should do so more nobly, and more enduringly.

Your rivalry as advisers on love-questions furthermore impels you to accept problems individually and to hand down private judgments. Be persuaded that this is a folly. Difficult love-cases, like accusations of serious crime, require the conjoined wisdom of a tribunal or jury. It was always so at Poitiers under our reign, and in succeeding centuries the Courts of Love in many a goodly palace in other lands followed the same pattern. Yet recall how you, Madame Ann, answered this missive from one of your correspondents. She wrote you:

I'm a girl 16, going steady with a boy 18. I want to break up with him but I don't know how. I had a slumber party at my house the other night and 14 girls offere[d] ideas but I don't think any of them are very good. I jus[t] hate to hurt this boy.—F.F.

This was your reply:

Dear F.F.: Strange that a tenderhearted miss should b[e] so insensitive to the boy's feelings that she would invit[e] 14 girls to submit ideas on how to unload him. Just te[ll] the fellow. Period.

"F.F.," it is to be feared, is more in the great traditio[n] than you. At Poitiers we always preferred a general dis[-] cussion and a collective decision; the graver the issue[,] the more voices we heard. Indeed, in a famous case con[-] cerning a go-between who treacherously made love to th[e] lady he approached on another's behalf, we gathered full[y] sixty ladies to hear the case. As a result, the condemnatio[n] of the go-between and the lady (both of whom were ex[-] cluded from the company of true lovers thenceforth) ha[d] exemplary force for centuries.

We deplore, too, what seems to be a strain of frivolit[y] in many of your decisions. To wit:

Dear Abby: Which is better? To go to a school danc[e] with a creep or to sit home? —All Shook Up

Your reply:

Dear Shook: Go with the creep, and look over the cro[p.]

We are somewhat perplexed by the elliptical rhetoric o[f] your remote era, but strongly suspect the answer to be [a] callow jape.

In many another instance, there is no doubt in ou[r] mind. In one case a young woman asked you, Ann:

Last night he said "I think we should get married o[r] something." Any advice?—Hoping

Your plainly flippant answer was:

Dear Hoping: You tell him you should get married— or nothing.

We also find a distraught letter to Abigail, as follows[:]

I am 32 years old and am old enough to know better[.] But Henry got me in a family way. I told him about i[t] and he said he would marry me. Then I had a miscarriage[.] Henry says there is no sense in marrying me now. Ca[n] you tell me what to do?—Violet

By MORTON M. HUNT

Abigail replied in this highly inappropriate fashion:

You are well rid of a man who would marry you only if he had to. Under the circumstances, I think you came out ahead. And by the way, you need one.

There were no such coarse jests in the decisions handed down by ourself and the ladies of our Court. We recommend to both of you, as a model of properly grave and moral writing on a love-question, the celebrated decision of our daughter Marie, Countess of Champagne, on a matter of great importance: "We declare and we hold as firmly established that love cannot exert its powers between two people married to each other. For lovers give each other everything freely, but married people are in duty bound to give in to each other's desires and deny themselves to each other in nothing. . . . Let this, our verdict, pronounced with great moderation and supported by the opinion of a great many ladies, be to you firm and indubitable truth." And as it happens, had such advice or such philosophy been brought to the attention of "Hoping" and "Violet," either of them might have been consoled about her situation.

It is possible, of course, that the defects in your language and thinking are in part the result of the tawdry circumstances in which you sisters consider love-cases—namely, amidst the clacking of a typewriter, the acrid cigarette smoke, the lonely sandwich hastily munched at one's desk. Can Love be philosophically viewed in such wise? Consider that at Poitiers the great assembly hall of the castle would be thronged with ladies, trailing brocades and furs, and with knights, elegant in slashed sleeves and pointed shoon. For a while some *trouvère* would strike the lute and wring our hearts with a mournful *lai*, until at last, our souls attuned to the task, we would hear the advocates and try to dispute the issues wisely. Such, cherished ladies, is the milieu in which problems of delicacy and moment should be considered.

Your own milieu, alas, produces in you an enfeeblement of interpretive power. Both of you urge young people to beware of heavy "petting" on the grounds that it is likely to lead to consummation. Yet this is shallow and impoverished counsel. We at Poitiers recognize that only when temptation and the desire to possess beauty are greatest is the omitting of the final solace Love's noblest expression; this way of Love we called *amor purus*, and we urged it upon all who were worthy of it as a practice of the highest merit. Or observe the following case, in which a young woman wrote to Abigail as follows:

I have been dating a young man who means nothing to me. He says he loves me. I have told him honestly I like him only as a friend. I feel guilty letting him spend money on me but when I turn him down he cries and it breaks my heart.—Sorry For Him

You, Abigail, replied as follows:

Dear Sorry: Girls who go with men because "they feel sorry for them" usually wind up feeling sorrier for themselves. Send him on his way. He'll live.

This is not only shallow, but genuinely immoral, as it seems to us. Ourself in a similar case once ruled that a woman who had accepted the service and gifts of a man had no right to claim inability to feel love in return; virtue consists in the proper recompense of the lover and not in a weak-willed defaulting of the obligation. But how shall you perceive this to be so, in your immoral era?

Nor should you stoop to concern yourselves with questions about one's husband's false teeth, the shaving of one's legs, the control of body odor, pimples, or loss of hair. These are for lesser hands. You should address yourselves only to such nobler matters as the rules of testing faithfulness, the importance of keeping Love secret, the length and kinds of service which entitle a man to the nude embrace, and so on. The difficult steps to the attainment of desire are what improve the character of man, and this, rather than false teeth, is your real concern.

Yet we are not unaware of the difficulties under which both of you labor and in view of which you may be said to have acquitted yourselves passably. We are not unmindful of the vanishing of the nobility in your time, the dominance of lower classes, and the wretched effort to merge Love with marriage. These things I presume you cannot change. Surely it must be problematical to appear as an authority on the subject of Love in a day that so confines one's experience of it. We ourself were more spacious and zealous: as all the polite world knew, we had been the beloved of our uncle, Prince Raymond of Antioch, as also of our court troubadour, Bernard de Ventadour, and others—all this giving us vision and feeling. Your own imperfections, dear ladies, may in large part be traced to the inadequacy of your times. You have done the best you could amid limitations; is there any hope that these limitations may once again be lifted?

With this we conclude, always believing that the gifts of beauty and intelligence should be put to highest use in the service of Love.

Given this 18th day of March, 1960, from somewhere beyond our tomb in the abbey of Fontevrault.

Eleanor, *Regina*

ANDY WARHOL

MILL: 190

LEIBNIZ: 185

GROTIUS: 185

GOETHE: 185

PASCAL: 180

MACAULAY: 180

BENTHAM: 180

COLERIDGE: 175

VOLTAIRE: 170

LEOPARDI: 170

CHATTERTON: 170

NIEBUHR: 165

MIRABEAU: 165

ADAMS: 165

WIELAND: 160

TASSO: 160

POPE: 160

PITT: 160

MUSSET: 160

MELANCHTHON: 160

What kind of early life fosters exceptional mental growth? A study of twenty great minds points to two prime conditions—and leads to a startling conclusion in the last sentence of this article

The Childhood Pattern of Genius

By HAROLD G. McCURDY

Genius by any definition is rare. If we make lasting fame one of the requirements, as Sir Francis Galton did in his classic work, *Hereditary Genius,* it is very rare indeed, and we are reduced to studying it at a distance through biography. Now, biographies have their limitations; as Havelock Ellis noted, one may search through them in vain for the most ordinary vital statistics. Above all, they cannot be expected to yield information on those details of early life, such as nursing and weaning and toilet training, to which psychoanalysis has attached so much importance. When, therefore, one proposes, as I do here, to explore the question of whether there is some pattern of environmental influences operating on children of genius which might help to account for their later achievement, it should be self-evident that the question is necessarily adjusted to something less than microscopic precision.

On the opposite page are portraits of the twenty geniuses chosen for this study. To explain the principle of selection, I must go back to the list of one thousand compiled in 1903 by J. McKeen Cattell on the theory that the amount of space allotted in biographical dictionaries could be taken as an objective measure of true eminence. In 1926, Catharine M. Cox, in her monumental study of genius, culled from this list a smaller list of 282, her requirements being (1) that the attained eminence should clearly depend on notable personal achievement, and (2) that the biographical material available should be sufficient to permit a reliable estimate of early mental ability. Men born before 1450 were eliminated. By studying the childhood records of the 282 men in the light of modern intelligence-testing experience, Miss Cox arrived at estimates of their IQs. From her list I chose the twenty-seven whose IQ in childhood was rated at 160 or better, and after dropping out seven whose biographical information was not easily available, I arrived at the present list of twenty.

In studying the environments of these twenty geniuses, I do not wish to give the impression that original endowment is an insignificant factor. On the contrary, Galton's strong arguments on behalf of heredity appear to me to be well founded; and in this sample, the early promise of these very distinguished men cannot be disassociated from the un-

usual intellectual qualities evident in their parents and transmitted, one would suppose, genetically as well as socially to their offspring. It is upon a groundwork of inherited ability that I see environmental influences operating.

Considerable theoretical importance is sometimes attached to the chronological position of a child in the family. Galton comments that "the elder sons have, on the whole, decided advantages of nurture over the younger sons. They are more likely to become possessed of independent means, and therefore able to follow the pursuits that have most attraction to their tastes; they are treated more as companions by their parents, and have earlier responsibility, both of which would develop independence of character; probably, also, the first-born child of families not well-to-do in the world would generally have more attention in his infancy, more breathing space, and better nourishment, than his younger brothers and sisters in their several turns." There is an intuitive appeal in the argument, but Galton does not support it by any precise analysis of his data. Nor does my sample lend much support to the theory. The number of first and only children is about one-third, which is close to the statistical probability.

There may nevertheless be something about position in the family which is significant. Let us look at the seven who do not rank as first-born children or first-born sons. Coleridge was born in his father's old age and was his "Benjamin"; Voltaire, whose invalid mother was incapable of bearing any more children, was so sickly during the first year of his life that there was daily concern over his survival; Chatterton was a posthumous child, and the previous boy in the family had died in infancy; Mirabeau, although he had several sisters, was the first male to survive after the death of the first son; Tasso was the only surviving son, his older brother having died before he was born; Pitt was in the interesting position of being able to follow his father in a parliamentary career in the House of Commons because his older brother, having inherited the title, could not do so; and Musset, the second of two sons, was younger than the first by a significant span of six years. When we weigh these additional facts, the general notion of some sort of positional effect begins to reassert itself.

The twenty geniuses studied by Professor McCurdy are shown at left with their estimated IQs.

One way in which position in the family might favor development would be by giving the child a higher attentional value for the parents. Close examination of the biographical data leads to the conclusion that these twenty men of genius, whether because of their position in the family or not, did as children receive a high degree of attention from their parents as well as from others. In several cases it is clear that the attention exceeded that accorded to their brothers and sisters. Both very decided and very positive parental interest was displayed toward Mill, Leibniz, Grotius, Goethe, Pascal, Macaulay, Bentham, Coleridge, Niebuhr, Adams, Wieland, Pope, Pitt, and Melanchthon. Voltaire and Musset were far from neglected, but the attention bestowed upon them may have lacked some of the intensity of focus notable in the preceding cases. If any of the children suffered comparative neglect or abuse, they would be Leopardi, Chatterton, and Mirabeau. Thomas Chatterton had no father from the time of his birth, and the fathers of Giacomo Leopardi and Mirabeau were lacking in sympathy, or worse. On the other hand, Chatterton's mother and sister helped him to learn to read, saw that he went to school, and were good enough to him that his childhood promise to reward them with all kinds of finery when he grew up was fulfilled in the last year of his short life; Leopardi was provided with tutors and had access to his father's rich library; and Mirabeau, cuffed and persecuted as he later was by his erratic father, was received into the world with an outburst of joy and was always provided for educationally, even though the arrangement may have been savagely disciplinary.

Favorable parental attention may take the two forms of displays of affection and intellectual stimulation. There is strong evidence for both in most of the cases in our list. Remarkable indeed are the educational programs followed by Mill, Goethe, Pascal, Bentham, Niebuhr, Adams, Wieland, Tasso, and Pitt, under the encouragement, guidance, and powerful insistence of their fathers. Yet it is not the educational program itself which requires our notice so much as it is the intimate and constant association with adults which it entails. Not only were these boys often in the company of adults, as genuine companions, they were to a significant extent cut off from the society of other children.

Warm attachments to children outside the family circle seem to have been rare, and there are several cases of isolation within the family too. Yet it is within the family that most of the recorded intimacies between these geniuses and other children developed. Goethe, Pascal, Niebuhr, Macaulay, Voltaire, and Mirabeau experienced some intensity of affection for sisters, Musset for his older brother. Macaulay and Voltaire remained attached to their favorite sisters throughout their lives, becoming devoted uncles to their sisters' children; Goethe's and Pascal's affection for their younger sisters approached passion; and Mirabeau speaks of incestuous relations with his.

The reality and nature of the pattern to which I am pointing—the great dominance of adults in the lives of these children, and their isolation from contemporaries outside and, sometimes, within the family—can be appreciated only through a more detailed statement about each individual:

JOHN STUART MILL
(1806–1873)

Under his father's personal and unremitting tutelage, he began hard intellectual work before he was three. From a very early age he was given the responsibility of acting as tutor to his brothers and sisters. This did not increase his affection for them. In fact, he came to share some of his father's own antipathy toward them and toward his mother. He explicitly states in his autobiography that his father kept him apart from other boys. "He was earnestly bent upon my escaping not only the ordinary corrupting influence which boys exercise over boys, but the contagion of vulgar modes of thought and feeling; and for this he was willing that I should pay the price of inferiority in the accomplishments which schoolboys in all countries chiefly cultivate." And again: "As I had no boy companions, and the animal need of physical activity was satisfied by walking, my amusements, which were mostly solitary, were in general of a quiet, if not a bookish turn, and gave little stimulus to any other kind even of mental activity than that which was already called forth by my studies."

JOHANN WOLFGANG VON GOETHE
(1749–1832)

Throughout his childhood he was carefully and energetically supervised in his varied studies by his father. He associated frequently with numerous skilled and learned and eminent men in Frankfurt, among whom was his grandfather Textor. He enjoyed considerable freedom of movement through the city in the intervals of his studies, and he struck up several acquaintances outside the home among boys and girls; but these were certainly far outweighed by his adult contacts, and by his intimacy with his sister, who had much less freedom than he and who became increasingly embittered by the educational discipline imposed by their father. In his autobiography Goethe notes that he was not on friendly terms with a brother three years younger, who died in childhood, and scarcely retained any memory of the three subsequent children who also died young. How close he and his sister were may be gauged by these words regarding the aftereffects of his love affair with Gretchen, at about fourteen: "My sister consoled me the more earnestly, because she secretly felt the satisfaction of having gotten rid of a rival; and I, too, could not but feel a quiet, half-delicious pleasure, when she did me the justice to assure me that I was the only one who truly loved, understood, and esteemed her."

GOTTFRIED WILHELM VON LEIBNIZ
(1646–1716)

His mother's only child, he lost his father, a prominent university professor, when he was six. He retained two vivid memories of him, both of them expressive of the high esteem in which his father had held him. His mother, who died when he was eighteen, devoted the remainder of her life to caring for him. He lived at home, free from "the doubtful liberties, the numerous temptations, the barbarous follies of student life." Before he was ten his father's carefully guarded library was opened to him, and he plunged into its treasures eagerly.

HUGO GROTIUS
(1583–1645)

He was close to his father. He signed his early poems Hugeianus, thus joining his own name, Hugo, with his father's name, Janus or Joannes. At eight he reacted to the death of a brother by writing his father consolatory Latin verses. He had competent teachers at home and entered the University of Leyden at eleven; there he dwelt with a devoutly religious man who impressed him deeply. He was famous in the literary world very early, and received high praise from distinguished men. He sought his father's advice when he chose a wife. One would infer from the limited evidence that his association from early childhood was primarily with adults.

BLAISE PASCAL
(1623–1662)

He was so precious in the eyes of his father, after his mother's death when he was three, that, as the older sister tells us, the father could not bear the thought of leaving his education to others and accordingly became and remained his only teacher. At eighteen Pascal's health broke down from ceaseless application. He was frequently in the company of the learned men surrounding his father. His primary emotional attachment was to his younger sister, Jacqueline; her religious retirement strongly influenced his own religious development.

THOMAS BABINGTON
MACAULAY
(1800–1859)

He early became absorbed in books, but his studies were less obtrusively guided by his father and mother and other relatives than in the cases preceding. He was especially attached to his mother in early childhood, and at home among his brothers and sisters he was overflowingly happy and playful. A sister writes: "He hated strangers, and his notion of perfect happiness was to see us all working round him while he read aloud a novel, and then to walk all together on the Common." He was re-

luctant to leave home for school for even a day, and he was acutely homesick when placed in a boarding school at about twelve; there, though tolerated and even admired by his fellow pupils, he had little to do with them, living almost exclusively among books. The children at home passionately loved him.

JEREMY BENTHAM
(1748–1832)

His father kept him to a rigorous schedule of instruction in everything from dancing and military drill to Greek from a very early age. From seven to twelve he spent the winters at a boarding school, which he did not enjoy; during vacations at home, his schooling, under private tutors, was much more intensive. He was happiest on visits to his grandparents in the country, where he could talk to an old gardener or climb up a tree and read a novel. Too small and weak to win the admiration of his fellows, "he tried to be industrious and honest and noble and dutiful, finding that such a course brought praise from his elders." When the death of his mother desolated his father and himself, Jeremy "was just turned twelve, and was ready for Oxford, if a frail and undersized boy of twelve could be said to be ready for anything."

SAMUEL TAYLOR
COLERIDGE
(1772–1834)

His father, though unambitious in general and not very attentive to the education of his numerous other children, took special pride in him and endeavored from the beginning to prepare him for the church. Coleridge was the last of fourteen children (ten by his mother), and his parents' extreme fondness for him aroused the hostility of the older boys toward him. They drove him from play and tormented him. On one occasion, when he was eight, he ran away from home after a ferocious combat with the brother whom he had displaced as baby of the family; he was found only after a prolonged search, and he remembered all his life the tears of joy on his father's face and his mother's ecstasy when he was recovered. The death of the father, when Coleridge was nine, deprived him of his most valued companion. Shortly afterward he was sent to a charity school in London. Here he made a few friends, notably Charles Lamb, but he lived a great deal in books and in his own imagination.

VOLTAIRE
(1694–1778)

He was born five years after the death, in infancy, of the preceding child, and his own life was despaired of daily for the first year. His mother was an invalid; his father was a busy lawyer and does not seem to have concentrated any particular attention on him, beyond desiring that the boy should be prepared for the law. His education at home proceeded under the guidance of three distinguished and learned men, particularly the Abbé Chateauneuf, his godfather. The two other surviving children were considerably older than he; the brother he disliked, but he was fond of his seven-year-older sister and, after his mother's death when he was seven, it was she to whom he was chiefly attached in the family. At ten he was sent to the best Jesuit school in France by his ambitious and wealthy father; here he made the warmest and most lasting friendships in his life, but they were with the teachers rather than with the boys.

GIACOMO LEOPARDI
(1798–1837)

He was the oldest of five children, and until he was twenty-four, he remained practically immured in the house of his father, the Count, in a town which he despised. In Leopardi's own words: "Had no teachers except for the first rudiments, which he learned under tutors kept expressly in the house of his father. But had the use of a rich library collected by his father, a great lover of literature. In this library passed the chief portion of his life, while and as much as permitted by his health, ruined by these studies; which he began independently of teachers, at ten years of age, and continued thenceforth without intermission, making them his sole occupation." His closest companion was his brother Carlo, a year younger, but he was reticent even with him. With the other children he liked to produce plays in which the tyrant (his father) was worsted by the hero (himself). At a later age he regarded his home as a prison from which he had to break out.

THOMAS CHATTERTON
(1752–1770)

Born three months after his talented father's death, he was the second surviving child of a very young mother, who had borne a daughter four or five years earlier, before her marriage was legalized. Under their instruction, he learned the alphabet from an old illuminated music manuscript of his father's, which his mother had been about to throw away, and learned how to read from an old blackletter Testament. He had been dismissed from his first school as a dullard. A note on his relations with playmates before he was five speaks of him as "presiding over his playmates as their master and they his hired servants." Already at five he was greedy for fame, and he asked that a cup which had been presented to him by a relative should have on it "an angel with a trumpet, to *'blow his name about,'* as he said." He did form friendships at school, one in particular; and the death of this boy plunged him into melancholy. But with none of these, or with his sister, was he intimate enough to share the secret of his Rowley poems, those impressive forgeries which seem to have been written under the inspiration and tutelage of the church of St. Mary Redcliffe rather than any human preceptor.

BARTHOLD GEORG NIEBUHR
(1776–1831)

His father, who had been a military engineer and explorer, took up residence, after his marriage at forty, in a small provincial town and devoted himself to his wife and family of two children. He liked to entertain his own and other children with stories, games, and music; but he concentrated particularly on the instruction of his son, for whom he also provided tutors from the age of four or five. A neighbor, Boje, who was editor of a literary periodical, took much interest in the boy; and Boje's wife began his instruction in French. Her death when he was ten overwhelmed him with grief and inclined him even more seriously to his studies.

MIRABEAU
(1749–1791)

The first surviving son of a family of the nobility, he was in the beginning his father's pride. Later, after disfigurement by smallpox at three and displacement from the position of only son by the birth of a brother when he was five, he became increasingly the object of his erratic father's dislike. Intense marital discord made him seem the more hateful because he resembled his mother's side of the family. He was unfavorably compared with the other children and was repeatedly put under severe disciplinarian tutors. Eventually, and more

than once, his father had him imprisoned. In the face of this persecution, Mirabeau, helped partly by the affectionate interest of an uncle, nevertheless succeeded in developing an extraordinarily winning manner in speech and personal contacts, even charming his jailers into relaxing their punishments. Whether or not he was inclined to solitude, it was forced on him by his father; much of his learning and literary production took place in prisons or their equivalents. He was highly erotic and may have had sexual relations with his younger sister, for so he asserts.

JOHN QUINCY ADAMS
(1767–1848)

He regarded his name as a perpetual admonition to live nobly. The Revolutionary War and the Battle of Bunker Hill, which he witnessed, confirmed a serious habit of mind from early childhood. As his father was often absent from home, his mother came to depend upon him when he was still a boy. His education began at home under a tutor, and it continued in Europe in the company of his father and other men notable in the governmental service. It was not until he entered Harvard that he attended a regular school for any length of time.

CHRISTOPH MARTIN WIELAND
(1733–1813)

He was educated at home under the eyes of his father, a pastor, in somewhat the same severe manner as was Goethe. He studied hard from the age of three. He says of his childhood: "I was deeply in love with solitude and passed whole days and summer nights in the garden, observing and imitating the beauties of nature." Prior to age seventeen, says his biographer, "we encounter not a single friend of his own age, only books and those who helped with them." He was sensitive and unsociable when away at school, and when he returned home he lived alone or associated with older men.

TORQUATO TASSO
(1544–1595)

His old father was often compelled to be away from home, leaving him with his young mother and his sister until, at the age of ten, he was separated from them forever and sent to join his father at the court of his patron prince. Even while he remained at home he was being strictly educated, first by an old priest and then in a Jesuit school which he loved. His mother, of whom he was pas-

sionately fond, died two years after he went to join his father. Of his childhood, his biographer, Boulting, says: "The prolonged absences of his father, the tears of his mother, the straitened circumstances and this sudden death were not healthy influences for a sensitive lad, and there was a great deal too much educational pressure put upon him. His father was proud of Torquato's talents and ambitious as to his future. He forced him on and took scudi from a slender purse to pay for special lessons in Greek. But a cousin came to Rome from Bergamo to share in Torquato's studies. No bookworm was this lad, but full of fun and a thorough boy. Nothing could have been luckier." A little later he had as his companion in the study of the graces (horsemanship, jousting, etc.) a boy of eight, son of Duke Guidobaldo. Otherwise he seems to have associated primarily with men, often men of great dignity and learning.

ALEXANDER POPE
(1688–1744)

The only child of his mother (there was a half-sister more than nine years older), he was from the earliest period a domestic idol. His father and mother, both forty-six at his birth, and a nurse concentrated their affections upon him, which must have become all the more intense when he grew sickly, and humpbacked like his father. "The [Roman Catholic] religion of the family made their seclusion from the world the more rigid, and by consequence must have strengthened their mutual adhesiveness." Most of his education was accomplished at home, with some help from a family priest and his father, who corrected his early rhymes. From the age of twelve he threw himself into his studies so passionately that his frail constitution threatened to break down.

WILLIAM PITT
(1759–1806)

He was born at the peak of his father's career as Prime Minister of England. When the title of Earl of Chatham was conferred on him, this second son, then seven, exclaimed: "I am glad that I am not the eldest son. I want to speak in the House of Commons like Papa." Partly because of his feeble health, the boy was brought up at home under the instruction of his father and a tutor. His father concentrated upon developing his son's oratorical powers. At fourteen he was sent to Cambridge, where he was placed in the care of a sound scholar who remained his inseparable companion, and practically his only one, for more than two years. He had no social life there. He read with facility such books as Newton's *Principia* and the obscurest of the Greek poets. According to Macaulay, "Through his whole boyhood, the House of Commons was never out of his thoughts, or out of the thoughts of his instructors."

ALFRED DE MUSSET
(1810–1857)

The second son in a family devoted to literature, he was "an infant prodigy on whom the intelligence of his brother, six years his elder, did not fail to exercise a stimulating effect. Alfred developed his mind in the constant companionship of Paul much more rapidly than he would have in the company of children his own age." He was notable from early childhood for his sensitivity, charm, emotional ardor, dramatic power, and susceptibility to feminine beauty. At a tender age he was already disappointed in love. He went to school briefly with his brother, but sickness and the hostility of the other children toward these Bonapartists soon led to their being tutored at home by a young man who knew how to combine pleasure with instruction.

MELANCHTHON
(1497–1560)

He always remembered the dying injunction of his father: "I have seen many and great changes in the world, but greater ones are yet to follow, in which may God lead and guide you. Fear God, and do right." Before this time (his father died when he was eleven) he was, by his father's express wishes, strictly educated, for a while in a local school and then by a tutor, a conscientious teacher and stern disciplinarian. Afterward he came more directly under the influence of the celebrated scholar Reuchlin, who was his relative. Of his earlier childhood it is related that he often gathered his schoolfellows around him to discuss what they had been reading and learning, and his grandfather delighted to engage him in learned disputes with traveling scholars, whom he usually confounded.

These brief sketches tend, I believe, to confirm the rule that children of genius are exposed to significantly great amounts of intellectual stimulation by adults and experience very restricted contacts with other children of their own age. Nor should we overlook the fact that books themselves, to which these children were so much attached, are representatives of the adult world. This is true not only in the superficial sense that they are provided by adults and, more significantly, may be drawn from a father's sacred library (one thinks of Leibniz, Leopardi, even Chatterton); but it is true in the profounder sense that they are written by adults and, in the case of most of the reading done by these children, for adults. Books extend the boundaries of the adult empire.

In this constant intercourse with the adult world there may be an effect especially important in the development of genius. Not only is there an increase of knowledge, which is the usual aim of the instructors, there is also, in many cases, a profound excitement of imagination. Even John Stuart Mill confesses that he did not perfectly understand such grave works as the more difficult dialogues of Plato when he read them in Greek at seven. What, then, happens to such adult material pouring into the child's mind? Mill does not elucidate his own case, but there is evidence in a number of the biographies that the dynamic processes of fantasy go to work on it and richly transform both what is understood and what is not.

Much of Goethe's association with other children was simply an occasion for expressing his vivid fantasy life; he entranced them with stories of imaginary adventures. Musset, also, reveled in a world of make-believe based upon the Arabian Nights and similar literature and bewitched his enemies by the magic power of imagination. These were to become poets. But Bentham, who was no poet, imagined himself growing up a hero, like Fénelon's Telemachus, and was stirred to moral fervor by sentimental novels. And two of the practical politicians on the list, Pitt and Niebuhr, may give us some insight into the process.

When Pitt was thirteen or fourteen he wrote a tragedy, about which Macaulay said: "This piece is still preserved at Chevening, and is in some respects highly curious. There is no love. The whole plot is political; and it is remarkable that the interest, such as it is, turns on a contest about a regency. On one side is a faithful servant of the Crown, on the other an ambitious and unprincipled conspirator. At length the King, who had been missing, reappears, resumes his power, and rewards the faithful defender of his rights. A reader who should judge only by the internal evidence, would have no hesitation in pronouncing that the play was written by some Pittite poetaster at the time of the rejoicings for the recovery of George the Third in 1789." Out of his learning Pitt had constructed a dream prescient of his own future career. And who can say that the actions of a prime minister are not so much the expression of a private drama as they are the realistic application of the sciences and the laws?

Niebuhr, who became a practical man of business and politics as well as the historian of Rome, writes explicitly about his own childhood experience in a letter to Jacobi in 1811: "Our great seclusion from the world, in a quiet little provincial town, the prohibition, from our earliest years, to pass beyond the house and garden, accustomed me to gather the materials for the insatiable requirements of my childish fancy, not from life and nature, but from books, engravings, and conversation. Thus, my imagination laid no hold on the realities around me, but absorbed into her dominions all that I read—and I read without limit and without aim—while the actual world was impenetrable to my gaze; so that I became almost incapable of apprehending anything which had not already been apprehended by another—of forming a mental picture of anything which had not before been shaped into a distinct conception by another. It is true that, in this second-hand world, I was very learned, and could even, at a very early age, pronounce opinions like a grownup person; but the truth in me and around me was veiled from my eyes —the genuine truth of objective reason. Even when I grew older, and studied antiquity with intense interest, the chief use I made of my knowledge, for a long time, was to give fresh variety and brilliancy to my world of dreams."

My point is that fantasy is probably an important aspect of the development of genius, not only in those cases where the chief avenue to fame is through the production of works of imagination in the ordinary sense, but also in those where the adult accomplishment is of a different sort. Instead of becoming proficient in taking and giving the hard knocks of social relations with his contemporaries, the child of genius is thrown back on the resources of his imagination, and through it becomes aware of his own depth, self-conscious in the fullest sense, and essentially independent.

There is danger, however, in the intense cultivation of fantasy. If it does not flow over into the ordinary social relations by some channel, if it has to be dammed up as something socially useless, then it threatens life itself. An expression of what I am referring to is given in that powerful scene in the first part of Goethe's *Faust* where the physician-magician, tampering with incantations, raises a spirit of overwhelming presence and quails before him.

Something nearer to an outright demonstration is furnished by the life of Chatterton and his suicide. Before he was eighteen, Chatterton was dead by his own hand. If we examine his life, we see that it breaks apart into two distinct regions: an outer shell of schoolboy, apprentice, pretended antiquarian, and writer of brittle satire; and a core—the serious and deeply emotional fifteenth-century poet Rowley, whose connection with himself he never publicly acknowledged. One must not forget that Chatterton's fantasy existence as Rowley has points of contact with his father, the musician-schoolteacher who died before his son was born but who, in a sense, presided over the boy's education through the music manuscript from which he learned his letters and through the blackletter Testament in which he learned to read. Moreover, through his father's connection with the magnificent church of St. Mary Redcliffe, which overshadowed the place of Chatterton's birth and became his favorite resort from the brutalities of Bristol, the imaginative boy might surely continue to hold converse with his father. The Rowley poems, furthermore, are related to Chatterton's search for a pedigree. In short, through Rowley, Chatterton established relations with the world of the dead. And since he could not admit that he himself was the author of the Rowley poems, but had to pretend to have found them in his role as antiquary (a pretense which prompted Walpole to call him an impostor), Chatterton, as Rowley, was unable to establish contact with the world of the living. The surface which he presented to the world was hard, brittle, violent, unreal. Yet even in his relations with the world, he appeared to be doing the same thing he was

doing through the Rowley fantasies; namely, seeking a father to love and protect him. He evidently placed great hopes in Walpole; but he had also tried and been disappointed in the patronage of men of lower caliber in Bristol. Eventually he came to a dead end in London, where he had no friends even of the quality of Bristol's Catcott. Just before he committed suicide, Chatterton became Rowley once again in the most beautiful of his poems, the "Balade of Charitie," which sums up his experience of the world and his yearning for a loving father. If it was Rowley who enabled him to live, it was also Rowley who opened the door of death and ushered him out of a world of constant, bitter disappointment into a world of kindly and Christian spirits.

Chatterton is a supreme example of the dangers and costs of genius. Having no father or other appreciative adult to link him to the world, he was swallowed up by his imagination. But it is too often overlooked in the textbooks that genius, even in less tragic cases, is generally a costly gift. Superficially an enviable piece of luck, it is actually a fatality which exacts hard tribute from the possessor. Extreme absorption in very hard work and, sometimes, broken health are among the penalties. Isolation from contemporaries, often increasing with the years, is another. Whether we should include heterosexual difficulties as another, I am not sure. Fifty-five per cent of our sample did not marry at all. Some delay or reluctance or dissatisfaction attended the marriages of Mill, Goethe, Coleridge, Mirabeau, Wieland, and perhaps Melanchthon, but it is not desirable here to go into greater detail because of the impossibility of making appropriate comparisons. It may be that for marriages both freely contracted and happily sustained a rate of three in twenty is not out of the ordinary, though I should be inclined to say that here, too, we have an expression of the costliness of genius.

In summary, the present survey of biographical information on a sample of twenty men of genius suggests that the typical developmental pattern includes as important aspects: (1) a high degree of attention focused upon the child by parents and other adults, expressed in intensive educational measures and, usually, abundant love; (2) isolation from other children, especially outside the family; and (3) a rich efflorescence of fantasy as a reaction to the preceding conditions. It might be remarked that the mass education of our public school system is, in its way, a vast experiment on the effect of reducing all three factors to a minimum; accordingly, it should tend to suppress the occurrence of genius.

Harold G. McCurdy, professor of psychology at the University of North Carolina, is the author of The Personality of Shakespeare: A Venture in Psychological Method *(Yale, 1953). His article is based on a paper published first in the* Journal of the Elisha Mitchell Scientific Society *and later in a report of the Smithsonian Institution.*

WHERE THE ROMANS ENJOYED "OMNIA COMMODA"

Bodily immersion is rudimentary today compared to the "every convenience" offered to the patrons of the world's most luxurious bathing establishments

By LAWRENCE WRIGHT

Wide-span roofs of the past tell us one important thing about the people who built them. The activity or utility that they thought deserved a great enclosed space, and to the roofing of which they devoted huge technical effort, is likely to have been their main interest in life. Today it is the aircraft hangar, with an even greater span than the exhibition hall or the cinema. In the nineteenth century it was the railway station; in the eighteenth century the noble mansion; in the Middle Ages the cathedral. In Rome it was the public bath. Here was the focus of communal life. Bathing was a basic social duty. The highest architectural and constructional skills were devoted to its setting.

The colossal scale of these baths is difficult to grasp. The Baths of Caracalla covered a site about 1,100 feet square, more than six times the area of St. Paul's Cathedral, and could take 1,600 bathers at a time. The Baths of Diocletian are said to have had twice this capacity; one room alone sufficed Michelangelo for conversion into the great church of Santa Maria degli Angeli.

Rome was supplied with water by thirteen aqueducts, of which the longest ran for about fourteen miles. Knowing tourists often point out that all this masonry was quite unnecessary, and that the silly Romans should have known that water finds its own level: a pipe run across the valley would have served. But the Romans were not so ignorant of hydraulics; they simply had no suitable metal, such as bronze, in sufficient quantity to make such very large pipes. They well understood the relative costs of materials and labor.

The remaining overhead aqueducts have made such a dramatic impression on travelers that it is not generally realized that the course of the Roman aqueducts was mainly underground. About A.D. 52 the total length of the eight main aqueducts was about 220 miles, of which only about 30 miles ran above ground.

In the fourth century A.D., Rome had 11 public baths, 1,352 public fountains and cisterns, and 856 private baths. Some private houses at Pompeii had as many as 30 taps. As well as private water-flushed latrines, there were plenty of public ones: Rome in A.D. 315 had 144, in Puteoli there was one for every 45 persons, and in Timgad one for every 28.

At the peak, Rome supplied 300 gallons of water per head per day. In London today about 51 gallons per head are used each day, of which 34 are for domestic and 17 for trade use, and in New York City the daily total is just under 150

At the magnificent Baths of Caracalla, men and women of Rome soaked themselves—often for hours each day—in great halls decorated by the finest artists of the Empire. Above, a reconstruction of the frigidarium, which was open to the sky.

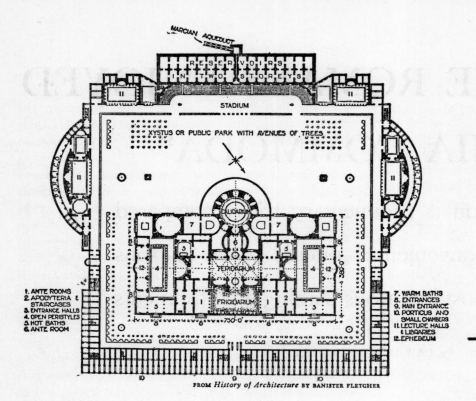

FROM *History of Architecture* BY BANISTER FLETCHER

1. ANTE ROOMS
2. APODYTERIA &
   STAIRCASES
3. ENTRANCE HALLS
4. OPEN PERISTYLES
5. HOT BATHS
6. ANTE ROOM

7. WARM BATHS
8. ENTRANCES
9. MAIN ENTRANCE
10. PORTICUS AND
    SMALL CHAMBERS
11. LECTURE HALLS
    & LIBRARIES
12. EPHEBEUM

Public baths were to Rome what cathedrals were to Europe's cities during the Middle Ages—hubs of social activity. Around the three main halls of the Baths of Caracalla (left) were a park, stadium, and lecture rooms. The total area was immense: compare that of St. Paul's Cathedral, London (below).

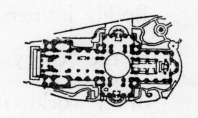

gallons. The Romans must have wasted more than we do, but even so they must have used more, especially for bathing.

The Roman bath drill, with some variations, is as follows. When the *aes* rings to announce that the water is hot, at about one o'clock, enter and pay your *quadrans* or quarter of an *as* (about half a cent). Have a game of tennis in the *sphaeristerium* to get well warmed up. Enter the *tepidarium*, a moderately warm room, and sweat a little with your clothes on. Then undress in the *apodyterium* and get anointed. Remember Hippocrates' advice that "the person who takes the bath should be orderly and reserved in his manner, should do nothing for himself, but others should pour the water upon him and rub him." You may bring your own special oil and ointment if you wish, but do not expect soap. The oil may be mixed with African sand if you are very dirty, as when you have been working on your chariot. Next move into the *calidarium*, or hot room, and sweat liberally, then briefly and more profusely in the *laconicum*, a hot spot directly over the *hypocaustum*, or furnace, where the hot air is controlled by a sort of damper. Now have plenty of water poured over you. There are three taps for this water: warm, tepid, and cold, to be used in that order. These taps are connected so that as fast as warm water is drawn off it is replaced by tepid, and tepid by cold, a means of fuel-saving only lately introduced into modern furnaces. You are now thoroughly scraped with a *strigil*, a curved metal tool with a groove, to collect the surprising amount of matter that will be removed. You are sponged. Re-anointed, you may end with a plunge in the cold bath in the *frigidarium*, before strolling or sitting around to meet your friends. You will feel splendidly refreshed and may well remark on the sorry state of the dirty native British in that newly won island somewhere up north.

Hours at the baths were usually from 1 P.M. until dark,

though one of the later emperors had them lighted up at night. The bath was supposed to promote appetite, and some voluptuaries took one or more baths *after* dinner to enable them to begin eating again, which occasionally proved fatal. Some of the more effeminate emperors are said to have bathed seven or eight times a day. The last word in luxury were the *pensiles balneae* mentioned by Pliny, small baths, suspended by ropes from the ceiling, in which one could rock.

In early times the sexes did not mix, a father could not bathe with his son, and no respectable matron would go to the baths at all; latterly promiscuous bathing was common.

On the walls of Pompeii are still various advertisements, including one that announces the opening of new baths:

DEDICATIONE . THERMARUM .
MUNERIS . CN . ALLEI .
NIGIDII . MAI . VENATIO .
ATHLETAE . SPARSIONES . VELA .
ERUNT . MAIO . PRINCIPI .
COLONIAE . FELICITER .

To construe: there will be a dedication or formal opening of the baths, and the public is promised a slaughter of wild beasts, athletic games, awnings to keep off the sun, and perfumed sprinklings. These last (*sparsiones*) produced a *nimbus*, or cloud, of perfume to sweeten the spectators, all too necessary if they were such a rabblement as Casca tells of in Rome, who "hooted and clapped their chopped hands and threw up their sweaty nightcaps and uttered such a deal of stinking breath . . . I durst not laugh, for fear of opening my lips and receiving the bad air."

The method of spraying is supposed to have been some form of large syringe or other "rude engine." Another Pompeian poster reads:

THERMAE .
M . CRASSI . FRUGI .
AQUA . MARINA . ET . BALN .
AQUA . DULCI . JANUARIUS . L .

offering warm sea and fresh water baths. As provincial shopkeepers still like to have a London or Paris address, so the Latin provincials often added that they followed the customs of Rome. Thus the keeper of a bathing house at Bologna advertised:

IN . PRAEDIS .
C . LEGIANNI . VERI .
BALINEUM . MORE . URBICO . LAVAT .
OMNIA . COMMODA . PRAESTANTUR .

his baths being in the fashion of the town, and offering every convenience. There is another famous and somewhat enigmatic advertisement from Pompeii which reads:

IN . PRAEDIIS . JULIAE . SP . F . FELICIS .
LOCANTUR .
BALNEUM . VENERIUM . ET .
NONGENTUM . TABERNAE . PERGULAE .
CENACULA . EX . IDIBUS . AUG .
PRIMIS . IN . IDUS . AUG .
SEXTAS . ANNOS . CONTINUOS .
QUINQUE .
S . Q . D . L . E . N . C .

To translate: "On the estate of Julia Felix, daughter of Spurious Felix, are to let from the 1st to the 6th of the Ides of August, on a lease of five years, a bath, a brothel, and 900 (90?) shops, bowers, and upper apartments."

The seven final initials are said to mean "they are not to let to any person practicing an infamous profession," but this seems an odd clause where there is a *venerium* to let, and other erudites have seen in it *si quis dominam loci eius non cognoverit* and fancy that they can read underneath *adeat Suettium Verum*, translating it as: "if anybody should not know the lady of the house, he should apply to Suettius Verus," all of which shows just how scholarly scholars can be. They have also translated a Pompeian street sign showing two sacred serpents: it means COMMIT NO NUISANCE.

Wherever the Romans settled they built public baths; there are remains of small Roman baths in London, and of an impressively large one at Wroxeter (Uriconium). Wherever they found hot springs they used them, as at Bath (Aquae Sulis), where they began to build within ten years of the occupation (about A.D. 54).

Not only the rich were catered for; the infantryman, marching every mile of the way from Italy and grousing at the cold mists of Northumberland, might find a hot bath ready when the ranks broke. The fort of Housesteads, on Hadrian's Wall, had an elaborate system of stone water tanks, drains, a bathhouse that has yet to be fully revealed,

and latrines. A suite of bathrooms was provided for the barrack blocks. Surplus water from a tank flushed the latrines, and a tap allowed an occasional more thorough flush. The main latrine measures 31 feet by 16 feet internally. Along the two sides was a continuous trough, above which wooden seats were doubtless ranged.

Earthenware pipes (*tubuli*) were common. Those found in the kilns at Holt in Cheshire were tapered at the spigot end to fit into a large open socket. Wooden pipes were more rare. Lead pipes were usually oval or ovoid, of sheet lead formed into a tube and soldered. Some of the pipes to be seen at Bath are oblong in section, the seams being joined by turning over the edges without soldering. Others are triangular and joined by a leaden rib. A length of about 10 feet was normal. The *plumbarii* used lead from the Mendips, from Cumberland, and from Wales. They often marked the product with their names, or with the names of the owners; pigs of lead have been found bearing the name of Hadrian. An important pipeline would have a tank every three or four miles so that repairs need not interrupt the supply, as well as to control the pressure, a practice resumed in the Middle Ages. Fittings such as stopcocks were of bronze. Spouts usually took the form of animals' heads: dolphins seem to have been especially popular, and recur strangely in lands as far apart as Nepal and Java. The Romans had pumps: one made on the lines described by Vitruvius in the first century A.D. was found at Silchester, of wood with lead cylinder-linings, though bronze was the usual material.

We must remember that the Roman occupation was not a single episode, but covered a period about equal to that between Queens Elizabeth I and II. It seems incredible that a civilization so long established can have been so utterly effaced that its every art, custom, and habit of living vanished, leaving no visible trace but the decaying roads. The explanation must be that the Saxons, Danes, Jutes, and others who came to fill the vacuum did not come to rule and tax, but to destroy and supplant the natives. The Saxons seem to have disliked towns, and are supposed to have left London deserted. Even the earliest invaders do not seem to have occupied the Roman villas—perhaps they thought them haunted? They may not even have understood what the bathhouse was for. Probably they razed the buildings to the ground and then learned nothing, even from the piles of bricks; if the simple art of brickmaking could be wholly lost, as it was, the art of plumbing could hardly survive. When the legions marched away, they could not take their baths with them, but they might as well have done so, for all the further use that was made of them. As Lord Grey might have said, the taps were being turned off all over Europe; they would not be turned on again for nearly a thousand years.

Lawrence Wright, an English architect and artist, is the author of the new book Clean and Decent, *a history of bathrooms and hygiene through the ages, from which this is an excerpt.*

*"Portrait" of Anne Knish
by Arthur Davison Ficke.*

Emanuel Morgan,

Anne Knish,

and Elijah Hay

created

a literary sensation

when their work

first appeared—

and another

when the truth

about them became known

*Futurist sketch, by Ficke,
of poet Emanuel Morgan.*

The Spectral Poets of Pittsburgh

By WILLIAM JAY SMITH

In the autumn of the year 1916, magazine editors and reviewers of poetry found on their desks a new and quite unobtrusive-looking volume of verse of some sixty-odd pages. It was bound discreetly in gray with a design of two superimposed triangles, black on white on the front cover and white on black on the back, and bore the title *Spectra* in large black letters; below it, in smaller letters, were the words *New Poems*. Under the interlacing triangles were the rather odd and previously unknown names of the two authors, Emanuel Morgan and Anne Knish. On the title page was the subtitle, *A Book of Poetic Experiments;* the New York publisher was Mitchell Kennerley. There was no dust jacket and no biographical information on the authors. Such a modest volume might have been supposed to have passed unnoticed; but in literary circles it proved, on the contrary, to be something of a bombshell.

In her preface Anne Knish outlined the purpose of the book. She and Emanuel Morgan were exponents of a new "Spectric" theory of poetry. It was their aim "to push the possibilities of poetic expression into a new region—to attain

a fresh brilliance of impression by a method not so wholly different from the methods of Futurist Painting." This theory, said Miss Knish, had originated with Mr. Morgan; and in his experiments in the volume he employed only regular rhymed stanzas for "the best expression of his genius," whereas she (who in this preface, at least, seemed to have taken on the voice of authority for the movement) used only free verse. The Spectric manner might well employ either one, as long as the theme of a poem was regarded as a prism "upon which the colorless white light of infinite existence falls and is broken up into glowing, beautiful, and intelligible hues." Moreover, the term "Spectric" connoted not only "the after-colors of the poet's initial vision," but also "the overtones, adumbrations, or spectres which for the poet haunt all objects both of the seen and the unseen world."

Not all readers of poetry, however keen their interest, could follow Anne Knish's Spectric adumbrations (one reviewer indeed found the preface as "brilliant as a rainy midnight in the country"). But there was no doubt about the fact that before many months had passed the leading poetic groups of the day—the Vorticists, the Imagists, the Futurists, the Chorists—were all passé and the Spectrists had moved into the front ranks of the avant-garde. Edgar Lee Masters wrote that he thought highly of Spectrism, "an idea capable of great development along creative lines." Other poets and critics were equally impressed. John Gould Fletcher spoke of their "vividly memorable lines." William Marion Reedy in *Reedy's Mirror* hailed them in glowing terms. Eunice Tietjens, associate editor of *Poetry*, wrote of *Spectra* to Mr. Morgan on May 9, 1917: "It is a real delight!"

Who were these experimenters, and what did they offer that made them such a poetic rallying point? As around the leaders of any movement, whether in politics or poetry, a certain mystery gathered. What was unusual to begin with was that so esoteric a group should emerge from Pittsburgh, a city that had not exactly been identified with the mainstream of American literature. As to the backgrounds of the two authors, readers soon learned from newspapers and magazines that Emanuel Morgan had returned to his native city after twenty years in Paris. His primary interest, it was said, had always been painting until his friend Remy de Gourmont had turned him to literature; he had only recently begun to publish verse. Anne Knish was reported to have been born in Budapest, but had lived in recent years in Pittsburgh; she was the author of numerous critical reviews in European periodicals, and of one volume of poems in Russian bearing the Latin title *Via Aurea*. It was rumored that she was strikingly beautiful and excessively temperamental; and when shortly afterwards another young and hitherto unknown poet named Elijah Hay, "a briefless barrister," joined the group, Mr. Hay and Mr. Morgan were reported at knifepoint over the tempestuous Knish.

Whether or not the Spectric poems exactly followed the theory did not seem to matter—they were certainly lively enough. Anne Knish's emotional nature was evident in her work; indeed, some of her poems (the writers, disdaining titles, printed them as Opus this and Opus that with noticeable gaps between the Opus numbers) seemed scratched into the paper with talons rather than pen:

> *Skeptical cat,*
> *Calm your eyes, and come to me.*
> *For long ago, in some palmèd forest,*
> *I too felt claws curling*
> *Within my fingers . . .*

And even at the sight of so common a dish as frogs' legs, Emanuel Morgan could feel ecstasy (*Opus 9*):

> *When frogs' legs on a plate are brought to me*
> *As though I were divinity in France,*
> *I feel as God would feel were He to see*
> *Imperial Russians dance.*

Here were poets to whom intensity was all-important, writing as if convinced they would be around for some time.

Of this not everyone was so sure. Although Amy Lowell is said to have recommended the volume to a group of apprentice poets at Harvard, she appeared to be on the whole unimpressed. Certainly as the "fair Trotsky" of the Imagist revolution, as H. L. Mencken termed her, she was scarcely ready to welcome competition. The Boston *Christian Register* of April 12, 1917, echoed her doubts: "In the preface to this extraordinary volume in which the spectric method is outlined we find very little that is attractive to us." The New York *Herald* of December 29, 1916, referred to Spectric poetry as "daughter of Futurist poetry, a granddaughter of *vers libre,* and no relation at all to real poetry."

But whatever doubts were raised and whatever hesitations expressed, Mr. Morgan's humor and Miss Knish's imagery had made their point and were to gain more and more adherents during the course of the next year and a half. The Philadelphia *Public Ledger* of March 24, 1917, was of the opinion that the Spectrists would "not disturb the world of verse in America or set any river on fire unless it be the Monongahela when it is covered with oil scum"; but the sentiment slightly to the north in Newark, New Jersey, was quite different. There Thomas Raymond, Republican nominee for mayor, decided to avoid political issues and to limit his campaigning to readings of *Spectra* and Walter Pater; he won the election, and at his inaugural party read selections from the volume with special attention to the work of Anne Knish. Letters poured into Pittsburgh requesting the advice and opinion of Morgan and Knish on a variety of subjects; little magazines asked for the latest Spectric products. Harriet Monroe accepted several new poems of Emanuel Morgan's for publication in *Poetry*, thereby giving him the seal of approval of the official organ of the American poetic renaissance. In a letter to Morgan dated January 4, 1917, Miss Monroe wrote: "I like *Opus 102,* but a tiny poem or two would not be enough to give the flavor. If I could have about two pages the reader would have a chance to get it." Morgan complied and sent her four more poems.

One of the most influential and advanced of the little magazines was *Others*, edited in New York by Alfred Kreymborg and backed by Walter Conrad Arensberg, one of the first great patrons of modern art. *Others*, whose motto was "The old expressions are with us always, and there are always others," devoted a special issue in January, 1917, to the Spectric school. It opened with *Opus 344* by Anne Knish, the opus number apparently indicating the extent of Miss Knish's feverish poetic activity since her original publication. The number included, besides new work of Morgan's, the first published poems of Elijah Hay (bearing titles such as "Nightmare after Talking with Womanly Women" and "Spectrum of Mrs. X" rather than opus numbers). It con-

SPECTRA
New Poems

EMANUEL MORGAN
ANNE KNISH

*The plain face of a
literary bombshell.*

cluded with a "Prism on the Present State of Poetry" in which Morgan, Hay, and Knish spoke alternately, followed by a voice proclaiming with finality: *There shall be ashes.*

The poets received letters from correspondents of all sorts. To one such correspondent, Emanuel Morgan replied that Spectrism belonged to its time because "it intends . . . by means of laughter or other illumination, to send an enhanced X-ray through the skin to the lungs and liver and heart of life." Among Hay's correspondents was the poet William Carlos Williams who, apropos of the Spectric issue of *Others,* wrote that he preferred Morgan, Hay, and Knish in that order. "A.K.'s things suffer from too much theory," said Dr. Williams. "Morgan is well represented, you are uneven— good and bad, A.K. has some fine passages."

A critical symposium entitled *The Young Idea,* edited by Lloyd Morris and published early in 1917, paid special attention to the Spectrists. Morris had sent to a number of poets and prose writers a questionnaire on the current direction of American literature ("In a word, where does our literature stand today, and whither is it going?"), and had divided his authors into two groups—the Empiricists and the Romanticists. A number of the contributors in both categories touched on the Spectrists. The poet Arthur Davison Ficke, listed among the Empiricists, pointed out that the "eccentricities and absurdities" of the new schools were no worse than the "banalities and sentimentalities" of the old ones. He added that "in fact, the vigorous shock which some of these aberrations have administered to the moribund body of poetry is distinctly galvanizing." (As time would show, he was quite right.) Another of the Empiricists, the rising lyric poet Witter Bynner, wrote with equal tolerance, "The pattern of the so-called 'schools' of poetry will do no harm, I think; for they will freshen and diversify technique."

In his own contribution to the symposium, Emanuel Morgan limited himself to stressing the Spectric characteristic of humor. Anne Knish, although she began with some diffidence ("I do not know if I have a right to speak on this subject;

for American poets will resent perhaps the criticism of one whose native tongue is the Russian and who has written only one English book"), went on with characteristic clumsiness: "These are in American poetry days only of beginning; and I think those people know nothing of European literary history who speak so much of 'new, new, new.' "

But as the fame of *Spectra* spread, its directing forces, Miss Knish and Mr. Morgan, became increasingly mysterious. Reporters, critics, and aspiring poets called at their Pittsburgh address only to find that the two had just left for New York; those who tracked them down in New York discovered to their dismay that they had moved on to Chicago. True, Alfred Kreymborg had been heard to refer publicly and "with a real gleam in his eye" to Miss Knish's extraordinary beauty. But although many people had been in correspondence with them, few seem to have laid eyes on the pair or, for that matter, on the gifted Mr. Hay. Rumors began to circulate at literary gatherings and on college campuses that Miss Knish and Messrs. Morgan and Hay might be spectral as well as spectric, that they might indeed be three-thirds of a ghost and not exist at all.

A writer who had referred frequently to the Spectric school in the course of his lectures throughout the country was Witter Bynner, the young poet who had won praise for widely published poems since the appearance of *An Ode to Harvard* in 1907 and who was not identified with any particular "school." In an address before the Fortnightly Club at Chicago in May, 1916, he said: "Most of this schismatic poetry is nothing but rot. How one can take up his time with it is beyond me." He did, however, see a ray of hope in the Spectrists, samples of whose work had apparently already reached him before publication. Quoting Emanuel Morgan's *Opus 62,* which begins

> *Three little creatures gloomed across the floor*
> *And stood profound in front of me,*
> *And one was Faith, and one was Hope,*
> *And one was Charity*

he went on: "Now of course this sort of stuff isn't quite so hopeless as some of the other, but what does it mean?" Bynner was asking similar questions about the Spectrists nearly two years later on April 26, 1918, in a speech before the Twentieth Century Club in Detroit. Midway in his lecture, to his utter amazement, a young man stood up and asked simply: "Is it not true, Mr. Bynner, that you are Emanuel Morgan and that Arthur Davison Ficke is Anne Knish?" Mr. Bynner's answer was just as simple; it was "Yes."

"A direct and large lie was too much for me," Bynner explained later of his sudden confession. So, then and there, to the vast amusement of the audience, he related in detail for the first time the true story of *Spectra.* "Brush off the dusty form of Mr. Barnum's Cardiff giant, and put it away forever," said the Detroit *News* a few days later; "there is now revealed a greater boax than this." *Spectra* is indeed one of the greatest literary hoaxes ever perpetrated in America; and the story that Bynner had to tell was an incredible one.

In February, 1916, on the way to visit his friend and fellow poet, the late Arthur Davison Ficke, at Davenport, Iowa, Witter Bynner stopped off at Chicago. While there, he went with some friends to a performance of the Diaghilev Ballets Russes. During the intermission, after a performance of *Le Spectre de la Rose,* danced by Massine, Mr. Bynner discussed with his friends the absurdity of some of the recent poetry "schools." There were the Imagists and the Vorticists, of course, but had they heard, he asked—glancing at his program—of the "Spectrists," the new poets who had just appeared in Pittsburgh? *They* were the ones to watch. Bynner, who had just come from Pittsburgh and who had been thinking what a good idea it would be to found a new school himself and have some "fun with the extremists," found himself, with this chance but inspired conversational gambit, faced with a virtual *fait accompli.* He composed the first three poems on the train the following day, and on arriving at Davenport, set forth to Arthur Davison Ficke and his wife his plan for a burlesque. Ficke, who was just as irritated as Bynner by the "schools" of the moment and who also thoroughly enjoyed a good joke, entered immediately into the spirit of the occasion. That evening the Spectrists came into being. The first problem, before producing more Spectric poems, was to settle on the names of the alter egos who would appear as their authors. Bynner's choice was, he recalls, "lumberingly poetic—the first part of it being a suggestion of 'I hear Emmanuel singing' and the second a sound reflecting the German word *Morgen*—so that the rather misty idea was 'morning song.'" He visualized "Emanuel Morgan" as a middle-aged gentleman with a long square-cut beard. Ficke, remembering that he had seen in the culinary columns of some Sunday newspaper a recipe for the Jewish pastries called knishes, decided on "Anne Knish." He saw Miss Knish—or better Mrs., since she was probably divorced —as a Hungarian lady who, through wide experiences, had kept an open mind and a pure soul. In fact, so absorbed did the poets become in their assumed characters and in the constant composition and recitation of Spectric verse that Mrs. Ficke ordered them out of the house. They retired to a hotel across the river in Moline, Illinois, where, as Ficke put it, from ten quarts of excellent Scotch in ten days they extracted the whole of Spectric philosophy.

"Sometimes we would start with an idea, sometimes with only a phrase," Bynner has recalled, "but the procedure was to let all reins go, to give the idea or the phrase complete head, to take whatever road or field or fence it chose. In other words it was a sort of runaway poetry, the poet seated in the wagon but the reins flung aside." One of these runaway episodes was related by Ficke in an unpublished essay. One day lunching with the Fickes, Bynner purposely slipped off his chair and fell noisily to the floor, his motive being, said

A SPECTRUM OF SPECTRIC VERSE

Opus 118

If bathing were a virtue, not a lust,
    I would be dirtiest.

    To some, housecleaning is a holy rite.
For myself, houses would be empty
But for the golden motes dancing in sunbeams.

    Tax-assessors frequently overlook valuables.
Today they noted my jade.
But my memory of you escaped them.

ANNE KNISH

Opus 15

Despair comes when all comedy
    Is tame
And there is left no tragedy
    In any name,
When the round and wounded breathing
    Of love upon the breast
Is not so glad a sheathing
    As an old brown vest.

Asparagus is feathery and tall,
And the hose lies rotting by the garden-wall.

EMANUEL MORGAN

Opus 6

If I were only dafter
    I might be making hymns
To the liquor of your laughter
    And the lacquer of your limbs.

But you turn across the table
    A telescope of eyes,
And it lights a Russian sable
    Running circles in the skies. . . .

Till I go running after,
    Obeying all your whims—
For the liquor of your laughter
    And the lacquer of your limbs.

EMANUEL MORGAN

Elijah Cerebrates for Emanuel

If only my thoughts were dolphins, fat and free,
Untaught by morals and uncurbed by speech,
Fresh as the waves that tumble on the beach,
I could be gay, inconsequentially.
My thoughts are more like anchovies, I see
How rigid, tail in mouth, linked each to each
Immutably and logically they reach,
The present, past and future thoughts of me!

ELIJAH HAY

*Poets Witter Bynner
and Ficke about 1916.*

Ficke, the "commendable one of startling the attending waitress into violent hysterics." When order had been restored and as much as possible of the cheese *soufflé* removed from the dining-room floor, his hostess remarked sadly but patiently, "How terrible to entertain a lunatic!" Bynner, "with a shriek of voluptuous and joyous recognition," dashed immediately to his room, where in the person of Emanuel Morgan he wrote his renowned "Madagascar," which opens:

> *How terrible to entertain a lunatic!*
> *To keep his earnestness from coming close!*

Ficke was responsible for Anne Knish's preface and for the design of the cover of *Spectra*, which he said represented the "Love of the Triangles." When their manuscript was completed, the poets sent it off to Mitchell Kennerley, who had published them both under their own names. Kennerley, to their great astonishment, accepted it at once for publication, apparently (as Bynner remembers it) as a bona fide manuscript; and when informed of the real identity of the authors, he agreed to keep the secret.

The "Pittsburgh poets" had no difficulty making their own way in the world; but Bynner and Ficke soon found opportunities to help their brain-children on. In the summer of 1916, before the book's publication, Herbert Croly, founder of the *New Republic,* and Philip Littell, its literary editor, were dining in Cornish, New Hamsphire, at the house of Homer Saint-Gaudens, where Bynner was then living. When

the two men noticed the proofs of *Spectra* lying on Bynner's worktable, he feared that the end had come. He recovered himself in time to say, however, that this was an advance copy of a book which had been sent to him for comment. Both Croly and Littell, delighted to have happened on something so new and vigorous as *Spectra*, urged Bynner to review the volume for the *New Republic*. Naturally the latter took pleasure in complying with the request and even greater pleasure in collecting the fifteen dollars he was paid for his review hailing the work of Morgan and Knish.

The spectres which Ficke and Bynner had unloosed were to haunt them on more than one public occasion. Mrs. Corinne Roosevelt Robinson, the sister of Theodore Roosevelt, herself a versifier and an active member of the Poetry Society of America, frequently gave literary luncheons at her house in New York. At one such party, attended by John Jay Chapman, Edgar Lee Masters, and William Marion Reedy, Mrs. Robinson brought up the subject of *Spectra* and, producing a copy, asked Bynner to read selections from it. While Reedy (who had already been informed of the true identity of the authors) and Edgar Lee Masters (who had not) vied with each other in praise of the poems, Bynner strained every muscle to keep a straight face. He had been free to smile earlier, however, when, as Emanuel Morgan, he had received in a letter from Edgar Lee Masters the effusive commendation: "You have an idea in the sense that places do have an essence, everything has a noumena [*sic*] back of its appearance and it is this that poetry should discover. Any poetry that correlates gets over; and poetry which only gets the image and separates that from all other images loses much of the spirit and meaning. Hence to me Spectrism if you must name it is at the core of things and Imagism at the surface." (Bynner and Ficke threw dice to decide who was to retain possession of the Masters letter; Bynner won three times in succession, and it was his to keep.)

Originally it had been their plan to enlarge the Spectric school as the hoax gained momentum; indeed, it was necessary to do so in view of Anne Knish's published hints that there were others to be heard from. But Spectric verse proved to be more difficult to produce than one might have imagined; and the poets had to be sure that the friends whom they approached would be sealed to silence. It is Witter Bynner's recollection that Edwin Arlington Robinson made several unsuccessful attempts at writing Spectric verse, but Edna St. Vincent Millay, when let in on the secret, declined to participate. George Sterling, the San Francisco poet, volunteered to join up under the name of Yvonne Roux, a nineteen-year-old French girl born in Texas but "safely out of there." Sterling assumed, however, that ribaldry was the keynote, and his efforts at naughtiness fell flat.

With the deadline for the Spectric issue of *Others* only a few days off, the two poets, having failed in their search for disciples, found themselves together again at Davenport, Iowa. Once more they retired across the river to Moline, this time to the home of Marjorie Allen Seiffert, a well-known poetess of the Chicago school. Before dinner they explained their predicament to Mrs. Seiffert; she tried immediately and failed as the others had. The gentlemen then resorted to force, "part jolly, part desperate." "We had told our tale to her in her bedroom, where she was making further efforts to be Spectric," Bynner remembered, "and into it we locked her, determined that not until she had become Spectric should she emerge." While the party downstairs enjoyed cocktails and part of dinner, Mrs. Seiffert labored "almost angrily" until, from a succession of manuscripts she thrust under the door, Bynner and Ficke selected a number they considered worthy of inclusion in *Others*.

She chose the name Elijah Hay almost as soon as she was released from her imprisonment. With a cousin acting as scribe and go-between, Mrs. Seiffert—as Mr. Hay—carried on a correspondence over a period of months with Dr. William Carlos Williams, Alfred Kreymborg, and others. As their correspondence progressed, Williams's frank and open manner with Elijah Hay became at times too much for Mrs. Seiffert. "How unfortunate that men use such unladylike expressions in their letters to each other!" she wrote Bynner. She wondered also if Williams had not begun to suspect something. In any case, the exchange of letters appears to have developed a real bond between Mrs. Seiffert and Dr. Williams; when they met, even before the exposure of the hoax, they appear to have delighted in each other's company.

As the cause gained ground, the Spectrists often had the pleasure of being presented to themselves. Kreymborg, announcing to Bynner that he had persuaded the Spectrists to compile an issue of *Others*, personally assured him that the school was genuine since friends of his knew both the founders, and that Anne Knish was, of course, a devastating beauty.

Before the exposure in 1918, Ficke's spectral alter ego, Anne Knish, followed him to France during World War I and surprised him there in what constitutes one of the truly surrealistic consequences of the hoax. Ficke, a judge advocate wearing the uniform of a U.S. Army captain and "trembling with awe," breakfasted one morning with a brigadier general of the Regular Army, whom he had known slightly during peacetime. Their conversation turned to literary matters, and the general brought up the subject of *Spectra*. He asked Ficke if he supposed the book to be genuine or just a hoax. Ficke answered that, although many people whose opinions he respected took the volume seriously, he himself had always been inclined to suspect that it was fake. The general congratulated him on his astuteness and said firmly that he was quite right. Asked how he could be so sure, the general replied, "Because I myself am Anne Knish." Naturally Ficke then plied him with questions about the whole affair and begged him to reveal the identity of Emanuel Morgan, but the general declared that he was under oath not to do so. Ficke understandably described this encounter as

Drawing of William Carlos Williams from Emanuel Morgan's Pins for Wings, *1920.*

one of "the most deliriously happy hours I have ever spent."

By the autumn of 1917, word had begun to get around that the Spectrists might not be all they seemed. Not long after the publication of *Spectra*, when Bynner was lecturing at Madison, Wisconsin, Dr. Horace M. Kallen, then an instructor in the Department of Psychology and Philosophy at the University, asked him point-blank in private if he and Ficke were not Morgan and Knish. Mr. Bynner did not then answer "Yes" as he did later at Detroit, but the way he said "No" led Dr. Kallen to conclude that his suspicions were justified. The Spectrists had, in any case, been popular with the Wisconsin undergraduates, who had invented, as a take-off on them, the school of Ultra-Violet poetry, which they introduced in the January, 1917, issue of the *Wisconsin Literary Magazine*. The poems of "Manual Organ" and "Nanne Pish," which the magazine featured, were reprinted in *Reedy's Mirror*. Here is Manual Organ's *Blossom 34*:

> I wished for her smiling lips.
> She wanted my golden curls.
> I was a banker's son.
> But she was just "one of those girls."
>
> Oh, I wish I were a gnat's tail!

Parodying the parodists is even further removed from reality than criticizing the critics; and when the affair had gone this far, Bynner and Ficke saw that it was time to stop.

Once the hoax broke, the reviewers and critics who had not been taken in, or who had spoken of the Spectrists with caution, were among the first to announce how right they had been; those who had been deceived tried to cover up their steps as gracefully as possible. Lloyd Morris claimed to have been informed of the suspected identities of the Spectrists when reading final proofs of his book, *The Young Idea*, a critical symposium which included the opinions of Morgan and Knish as well as those of Ficke and Bynner, and to have gone ahead "with full knowledge." Harriet Monroe, who had accepted five poems of Emanuel Morgan's and one

47

of Elijah Hay's for publication in *Poetry*, now refused to print them. Miss Amy Lowell seemed relieved that the New Poetry, in her eyes the "most national" thing that America had to offer, along with skyscrapers and ice water, was still hers to command: Ezra Pound she had already dismissed and there *was* no Emanuel Morgan.

Others in the Spectric audience spoke up. Alfred Kreymborg maintained that the poems of Emanuel Morgan and Anne Knish were superior to anything that Bynner and Ficke had published under their own names. Another critic wrote that anyone familiar with Freudian psychology would realize that the writers had revealed the "*real* Bynner" and the "*real* Ficke" because they had let themselves go and had not permitted the "conscious censor" to intervene.

In the end, Ficke and Bynner were ready to admit that, to some extent, the joke was on themselves. Shortly after the disclosure, Bynner commented sadly that he could not get rid of Emanuel Morgan. "I find now that I write like him without the slightest effort—I don't know where he leaves off and I begin. He's a boomerang!" And much later, reviewing the whole episode, he said that some people still thought that Ficke and he had written better as Knish and Morgan, and added: "Once in a while we think so ourselves." To this, Arthur Davison Ficke's unpublished retort was: "This is inaccurate; we never think that, as applied to *our own* poetry; but we thoroughly think it about *each other's*."

The story of *Spectra* should end here; but, true to classical form, it must end where it began, and so it does. Very soon after the hoax broke in 1918, Witter Bynner, then a member of the English department at the University of California at Berkeley, received a letter from Candor, New York; it was signed by a certain Earl Roppel, and contained a sheaf of poems. The first one, entitled "Moon Light," was accompanied by the note, "This is one I wrote after reading your book":

> *Last night when I was in our surrey,*
> *Driving home with my best girl,*
> *I saw the moon run down the fence-row*
> *Like a fat squirrel.*

Another lyric commented on the impact of the war on the poet's pastoral existence; still another depicted his mother moving toward the kitchen door, "dirty water circling in her dishpan."

Bynner showed the poems to his colleagues on the University of California faculty, and they all agreed with him that they displayed a freshness and sincerity that Robert Burns himself might have admired. The prize poem of the lot was one that drew the special attention of Professor Arthur Farwell of the Department of Music. He promptly set it to music and later had it sung in San Francisco by a chorus of three thousand trained voices. Professor Farwell was quoted at the time as saying that the work, entitled

"Sunset," was the best patriotic song-poem in America:

> *Flag of our country, strong and true,*
> *The sky is rosy with your bars;*
> *But as they fade it turns to blue*
> *And radiant with your stars.*

> *And as I watch the setting sun,*
> *I call to God apart,*
> *"Give me the soul of Washington,*
> *And give me Lincoln's heart."*

Professor Farwell had gone ahead with his venture without the author's permission, but this seemed impossible to obtain, for Witter Bynner's letters to Earl Roppel in Candor were forwarded to a New York City address, from which they were returned marked "No such person." An inquiry of the library at Owego, ten miles from Candor, brought back the information that, to the best of the librarian's knowledge, no Earl Roppel had ever made use of that institution. When Bynner looked more closely at the New York address to which the letters had been forwarded, 186 Greenwich Avenue, he began to suspect that all was not right with the farm poet. Was it possible that some of his literary colleagues were taking revenge on him for *Spectra*? Was he, in turn, being hoaxed? He came to think that the culprit was none other than his good friend Edna St. Vincent Millay; but it was not until 1920, when an article signed by Malcolm Cowley appeared in the *Literary Review* of the New York *Evening Post*, that the truth was finally known about Earl Roppel of Candor, New York, the "bard of the rushing Catatonk."

Malcolm Cowley related how he and a friend, S. Foster Damon, finding themselves one afternoon in 1918 on the banks of the Catatonk, had sat down and composed the best of Earl Roppel's poems within an hour. The two men had sent the Earl Roppel letter and poems not only to Witter Bynner but also to Conrad Aiken and Amy Lowell. Although Bynner's letters were returned by the post office, the young men did receive Aiken's and Miss Lowell's. Both were taken in as Bynner had been, and Miss Lowell even volunteered to get some of Roppel's poems published in *Poetry*.

And so, as in a folk tale, was the trickster tricked; and what could have been more appropriate both from a literary and a democratic point of view than to have the very sophisticated Emanuel Morgan meet his match in a supposed country bumpkin? And what more classical irony could there have been than the fact that Malcolm Cowley, the man behind the mask, was *really* from Pittsburgh?

William Jay Smith has written a book about the Pittsburgh hoax (to be published later by Wesleyan University Press), three volumes of poetry, and four children's books. He is Resident Poet and Lecturer in English at Williams College.

it
all
began
with

B. B.
whose sudden fame
gave a group of young French film makers
their chance to launch

The New Wave

By HENRY B. DARRACH

On the terrace of a villa in the sunny south of France, a beautiful young blonde lay bottoms up and birthday-bare. Down swooped the camera, up swelled the blonde until she filled the mighty CinemaScope screen from end to end with the biggest and most sensationally popular post card that ever came out of France. In less than two years (1956–57) a relatively inexpensive quickie named *And God Created Woman*, starring Brigitte Bardot and directed by a twenty-eight-year-old unknown named Roger Vadim, grossed more than $4,500,000 and restored to Paris the World's Championship of Sex. That much might possibly have been foreseen. But who could have imagined that one blonde bottom would be in the forefront of an artistic renaissance of the French cinema that promises to become one of the most important cultural phenomena of postwar Europe? Yet it was Brigitte's big splash that started a ripple of innovation in French films; and it was that ripple, swelled by public protest, critical censure, government pressure, and the passion and talent of a handful of angry young Frenchmen, which at last rolled up the astonishing New Wave (*La Nouvelle Vague*) of creative vitality that in the last twelve months has crashed and

Alain Resnais's first feature film, Hiroshima Mon Amour, *tells the contemporary love story of a Japanese man and a French woman through shifting images of memory. In the scene below, she tells her lover,* "Bien sûr que je vais rester à Hiroshima avec toi."

swirled through the rickety film industry of France.

The Wave, by all reports, is getting wilder by the week. In 1959 a total of seventeen feature films were released by young French directors under the age of thirty—a number of them were actually under twenty-five—who had never before turned out anything longer than a short-subject. As the new year began, several dozen young and virtually unknown French directors were reported hard at work on their first full-length pictures. Few of the films so far released have cost more than $200,000.* And few of these pictures could budget a big star to catch the public eye. Some of them made stars of the actors and actresses they introduced —Jeanne Moreau, Jean Claude Brialy, Juliette Mayniel. Nevertheless, of those so far shown in the United States, at least three (*Le Beau Serge, The Cousins, The Lovers*) are fairly good films that emphatically promise better. Two others (*Black Orpheus, The 400 Blows*) are magnificent movies. And still another (*Hiroshima Mon Amour*), scheduled for United States release this spring, is generally considered one of the cinema's rare poetic masterpieces.

With such works to give it weight, the New Wave has swept through Europe with greater force than any film movement since the neorealist outpouring of postwar Italy. Last summer the "Beardless Wonders" carried off the big prizes at all the big film festivals—Cannes, Venice, Berlin. Overnight the New Wave shattered the "crisis of indifference" that had kept the "profitable margin" of French movie-goers dozing at home by the television set. Furthermore, for the first time in film history a mass public went to the movies to see a movie and not to see a star. "The Star system is broken!" cried one young critic, perhaps a little prematurely. "Today we have a cinema of directors. . . . The public rushes to see the latest film by Chabrol as it rushes to the latest play by Anouilh, the latest show of Picasso."

Last fall the New Wave broke with a satisfactory bang on the profitable shores of North America. *The Lovers,* which managed to get both a good press and an angry blast from the Legion of Decency, was soon well away to a multi-million-dollar *succès de scandale,* and, shortly thereafter, *The 400 Blows* was acclaimed by the New York Film Critics' Circle as the year's best foreign-language film. "The French film," cried a proud young *cinéaste* in Paris, "has been reborn from its ashes. It is France that will create the cinema of tomorrow."

But is it? So far, the New Wave amounts, in quantitative terms, to no more than a drop in the big bucket of world film production. And on the basis of three first-rate films, no national cinema can very confidently claim to lead the world in quality. Nevertheless, there are several reasons to suppose that the film in France may indeed be entering a golden age.

For one thing, the considerable film industry of Paris has created a large and skillful population of cinema technicians

*The average French film of the fifties cost about $300,000, while the average Hollywood feature is brought in for about $1,800,000.

—the know-how is there. For another, the industry is in desperate financial straits. During thirty years of cynical mismanagement, the fine films of such directors as René Clair, Jean Renoir, Julien Duvivier, Jacques Becker, and Marcel Carné have been exceptions. Now the front offices have, in effect, relinquished control of production to the creators themselves—a condition almost unknown, since the early twenties, in any film industry anywhere else in the world. Furthermore, the de Gaulle regime, as a part of its broad scheme to revive the arts in France, has set up a schedule of state subsidies that puts a premium on quality. (To qualify, a film must "serve the cause of the French cinema, open new paths in the art of the cinema, or make public, important ideas and problems of the French Union.") And finally, there is the New Wave itself—a mobilization of men and ideas that embraces considerably more than meets the eye on the silver screen. On the surface the New Wave seems only a bright froth of *cinémanes*, the sort of fellows who would cheerfully go to Hell to get a shot of the Devil. But beneath the surface runs the ground swell of a mass movement that has been rising steadily for more than twenty years, and has produced in contemporary France the first cinematically mature mass audience.

The movement began in 1936 when a young film enthusiast named Henri Langlois established in Paris a film library—much like the one later included in New York's Museum of Modern Art—and called it *La Cinémathèque Française*. The library quickly accumulated a formidable collection of old films and ran them off at regular showings, which soon attracted a large and fanatical following. After the war, the idea spread rapidly, much as the Little Theater movement had spread some fifty years before, and by the middle fifties, almost every two-horse town in France had its *Club de Cinéma*.

It was this *public connaisseur* that produced and now supports the New Wave of French directors. Converging on Paris from all parts of France, dozens of talented young men made *La Cinémathèque* their temple and the late André Bazin—in their opinion "the greatest, the only critic of his day"—their high priest. Roberto Rossellini (*Open City*), Federico Fellini (*La Strada*), Orson Welles (*Citizen Kane*), and Jean Vigo (*Zero for Conduct*) were the cinematic gods of the *Culte Bazin*. Honoré de Balzac, as one of the greatest of the French realistic novelists, was its literary idol. Some of the young men wrote for André Bazin's weekly, *Les Cahiers du Cinéma*, and the most brilliantly articulate of them, a twenty-eight-year-old reformed delinquent named François Truffaut, became the principal spokesman of his cinematic generation.

With sincerity, ferocity, and devastating elegance, Truffaut lashed out at the "boulevard intellectualism" and "employee mentality" of the established French directors, "these Merlins of the cinema, jealous of their power and their mystery." With soaring and romantic eloquence he enunciated the creed of the new cult of cinema: "It is necessary to film another thing in another spirit. It is necessary

Louis Malle, who directed The Lovers, *shocked many viewers with such scenes as the one below. Of his frank story about a latter-day Madame Bovary, Malle insists, "It is a moral picture. It shows a woman finding love in a desert of loneliness."*

Claude Chabrol wrote and directed The Cousins, *the story of the corruption and destruction of a decent youth from the provinces by his dissolute Parisian cousin. Below, they are seen the morning after a wild party, the city cousin somberly toying with his pistol.*

to abandon these expensive, ill-equipped, disorderly, and insalubrious studios. . . . The sun costs less than a battery of lights. . . . A borrowed camera, some cheap film, a friend's apartment, friends to play the parts, and above all the faith, the rage of the cinema—the rage to storm the barricade, the rage to use this way of expression—that is our way, the way of the future. . . . A revolution of intentions is beginning. . . . No longer do we trust in the old labels, the established themes. To express ourselves! Above all, to be free, free of prejudice, free of the old religion of technique, free of everything. Our generation is more simple, much more simple than the last, and above all more lucid. Only imbeciles take themselves seriously. . . . What matters is to be madly ambitious and madly sincere."

Truffaut's *copains* joined in the refrain. Grandly they announced that "the cinema of the last thirty years appears now as a mere stage of transition. . . . The cinema of today has come into the hands of the intellectuals, of the people who, under other circumstances, would have written novels. . . ." The new cinema, the young writers proclaimed, would be "a cinema of the author," in which the camera would be used as a pen. "The film must gradually free itself from the tyranny of the visual, from the image for its own sake, in order to become a means of writing as subtle and as supple as the written word." And what would the camera-stylo write about? It would write, *Les Vaguistes* proclaimed, of the things Balzac wrote about. "That is to say," one young scenarist explained, "about everything! About life as it is, people as they are. People with real feelings and real problems. Down with Formalism! Away with the Cult of the Beautiful!"

All this was, of course, much more than the victims of the new criticism could endure in silence. "Romantic amateurs!" they sneered. "Weekend cinematographers!" The theories of the New Wave, they agreed, were merely "daisy chains of self-congratulation" and "aggressive imbecility." *Les Vaguistes* were just a bunch of frustrated writers who wanted to make literary movies, and *La Nouvelle Vague* itself, they assured the public, was no more than a "retrospective revolution," on the whole "more *vague* than *nouvelle*."

Alas, the old-timers had to eat their words before the ink was dry. Brigitte bared her bottom, and French producers got the idea that the public wanted to see new bodies rather than old stars; they seemed also to respond to the angry, more or less beat view of youth by youth that B.B.'s first major exposure represented. And then, as fate would have it, an old man died leaving an $80,000 legacy to the wife of a twenty-five-year-old Baziniste named Claude Chabrol. Chabrol immediately took off for his home town in the Creuse to produce a motion picture. It was not a staggeringly good picture, but it was certainly new and different. The exhibitors snapped it up, and the government handed Chabrol a solid subsidy and told him to make another one. He did. Both pictures—*Le Beau Serge* and *The Cousins*—opened in Paris the same week, and to the amazement of all concerned they were both smash hits. At a thumb-stroke, as the French

say, the obscure and somewhat peculiar figure of Chabrol—
who looks, according to his friends, like "a slightly depraved
owl"—became the darling of the pigtail set and the culture
hero of the sidewalk cafés. And within a month, another big
fish came leaping out of the New Wave. Louis Malle, the
twenty-seven-year-old son of a beet-sugar magnate, borrowed some of daddy's sugar and made something rather too
sweet but undeniably skillful called *The Lovers*—a film distinguished by a long and splendidly photographed sequence
in which two young people (Jeanne Moreau and Jean-Marc
Bory) make passionate and naked love while the sound
track bellows Brahms.* *"L'amour passion!"* the critics
cried, and the public beat down the doors to see it. *The
Lovers* has made $360,000 in Paris alone, and the returns
are not yet in from the back country, where the film is still
showing.

Then in rapid succession came the three *chef-d'œuvres*
of the new dispensation:

The 400 Blows is the first feature film directed by critic
Truffaut, who was advanced the money ($110,000) by his
father-in-law, a wealthy producer whose turkeys the young
man had basted with vitriol. *"Eh bien,"* said Papa, "let's
see if you can do better." Truffaut did better.

His picture, made with little-known actors and a twelve-
year-old hero, Jean-Pierre Léaud, who had never before
faced a movie camera, tells a story suggested by Truffaut's
own childhood, part of which was spent in a reform school.
The hero is a Parisian schoolboy, lower-middle-class, with a
weak-kneed stepfather and a round-heeled mother. The boy
gets into trouble at school, decides in desperation to "do the
400 blows"—go for broke. He runs away from home, steals
a typewriter from his father's office, gets caught. His father
disowns him, turns him over to the police. Sent to a tough
reformatory, he runs away again. He runs and runs until he
reaches the edge of the sea, the end of his hope. There, with
eyes suddenly old in his decent young face, the boy turns
back to face a world he never made, a fate that the onlooker
suddenly recognizes as his own.

The film is indeed, as critic Truffaut promised, "madly
ambitious and madly sincere," but it is also painfully moving and amazingly wise. At twenty-eight, this vigorous and
intelligent young man has already put a remarkable distance
of experience between himself and his youthful revolt. The
foaming romantic has become a clear-eyed realist, the raging
intellectual a richly imaginative artist.

Black Orpheus is the work of Marcel Camus, at forty-
eight the *doyen* of the new school. After ten weary years as
an assistant to some of France's top directors, Camus got
sick of it all, dug up a nervous Maecenas, and took ship for

Marcel Camus's Black Orpheus *re-creates the classic
legend of doomed lovers in a
Brazilian setting. Below, Marpessa Dawn, who plays Eurydice, stumbles amid carnival
crowds of Rio into the arms
of Death in the guise of a re-
lentless and pursuing suitor.*

LOPERT FILMS

*Even more sensational, according to reports from Paris, are some
sexy scenes in Roger Vadim's production of *Les Liaisons Dan-
gereuses* (the eighteenth-century classic of love and mistresses by
Pierre Choderlos de Laclos, set in contemporary France), which also
stars Jeanne Moreau, along with the late Gérard Philipe and
Annette Vadim. The picture is being shown in France, but the French
government has been withholding an export license because it fears
that the film would give people the wrong idea about France.

François Truffaut won fame for his The 400 Blows, *the brilliant and heartbreaking story of a boy rejected by a callous society. Below, Jean-Pierre Léaud is seen at the moment when, disowned by his family, he is jailed for the theft of a typewriter.*

Brazil. There, with an all-Negro cast of amateurs and unknown actors, he began to film an adaptation, in Portuguese, of the Orpheus legend among the celestially beautiful hills around Rio de Janeiro.

Alas, no money came from France, and after a couple of months Camus, having hocked everything but the film he had shot, started sleeping on the beach. "The poverty in the long run was not such a bad thing. I spent so much time trailing around on foot, just looking, that in the end I had a deep awareness of Brazil. With money I would never have made the same film. Everything would have been done too quickly." Down to his last seventeen dollars, Camus was rescued by none other than the president of Brazil, Juscelino Kubitschek, who ordered the Brazilian Army to lend Camus the necessary supplies.

Camus's picture tells the story of a young Negro streetcar conductor named Orfeo (played by Breno Mello, a Brazilian *futebol* player), who meets a soulfully beautiful country girl called Eurydice (played by Marpessa Dawn, a dancer from the vicinity of Pittsburgh, Pennsylvania) at the start of the carnival season, and falls in love with her. But Eurydice is pursued by a sinister stranger in a black domino, and in the gaudy night of the carnival he haunts her down to her death. Seeking his Eurydice at the Bureau of Missing Persons, then at a morbid rite where spirit rappers raise her ghost, Orfeo wanders, singing his grief. In the end, Eurydice's rival, screaming like a Fury, sends the brokenhearted Orfeo to join his love in death.

The film is a stunning thing. Visually, it is a Joseph's coat of brilliant colors, spectacularly stained with blood. Technically, it is crude, splurgingly careless, grandly imperfect as life itself is imperfect. Rhythmically—and essentially, this film is nothing but rhythm—it is a violent ballet of images, a dance of life that every minute whirls more wildly, as the pounding drums accelerate the carnival's chthonian delirium.

Hiroshima Mon Amour, which is proclaimed in France as the high-water mark of the New Wave, is the first full-length picture by the thirty-eight-year-old Breton, Alain Resnais. He had previously made a minor international reputation as a creator of fine documentary films: *Van Gogh,* a short-subject released in the United States in 1950, won one of Hollywood's Oscars, and *Night and Fog,* a harrowing study of the German concentration camps, is a classic of its dreadful kind. Resnais himself is a shy, intense, passionately humane man of the noncommunist Left. He lives quietly, avoids people except for a few close friends, and is said to work slowly but with a will of iron.

In *Hiroshima* director Resnais takes two characters and describes a night in their lives—and their lives in that night. He (Ejie Okada) is a Japanese architect; she (Emmanuelle Riva) is a French actress. They meet in present-day Hiroshima, fall in love at first sight, spend the night together. But they cannot forget that they are making love in a mass grave, in the crater of a spiritual catastrophe. He tells her about the Bomb, what it did to the people he knew, what it did to him. She tells him about a personal disaster in her own past. During the years of Occupation she had fallen in love with a German soldier, had seen him killed, had suffered the brutality of "national disgrace," had gone insane, and had finally escaped to Paris.

By all accounts, the film is exquisitely played and photographed, and Resnais has subtly interfused his several schemes of time, one present and two past, into a permanent, poetic present in which everything matters because everything is possible—even the redemption of the past. "The freedom with which Resnais has handled this part of the film," one critic has written, "is probably without parallel in the history of cinema." The film's fine artistry has mattered less to most critics than its spiritual force. Alain Resnais seems to project an image of Hiroshima not only as a fateful common ground, where men and nations may meet to be reconciled, but also as a monstrous and sacred tomb, which may be witness to the miraculous salvation of mankind.

With these accomplishments behind them by the late spring of last year, the New Wave hung in the balance. The weight of popular approval was behind it, but the money men were set to throw up the barricades. Suddenly the government stepped in. Over the protest of "the big vegetables" in the French film industry, André Malraux, Minister for Cultural Affairs, selected the three best films of the New Wave to represent France at Cannes in 1959. France swept the festival. *Black Orpheus* was honored as the year's best film, Truffaut was voted the best director, and *Hiroshima Mon Amour* won the International Film Critics Prize in the "Special Category." Emboldened by such success, seventeen young cinema lions met in a Riviera hotel to roar a manifesto at the *ancien régime:*

(1) the film is a vocation, not a trade;

(2) we demand complete freedom and choice and interpretation of subject;

(3) we refuse to be labeled avant-garde;

(4) we challenge the industry to compete with us in the open market and to let the public decide who is right.

With that the industry's resistance caved in. All over Paris hard-lipped producers rushed to lay their fortunes at the feet of beardless boys bearing 16mm cameras, whereupon, of course, the Cassandras raised their doleful chorus: "The danger is success. The producers will offer them more money to make better films. The danger is the second or third film." But Resnais thought otherwise. "The best is yet to come. It will be people far younger than we, people not yet heard from, who will make the true revolution." And Malle was heard to crow: "We've won. The world is our oyster. We're on the march. Nothing can stop us."

Marcel Carné, an old wave master (Children of Paradise) *decided that he would join the New Wave and turned out* Les Tricheurs (The Cheats), *a slick study of the Paris chapter of the cool-jazz, change-partners Beat Generation. Below, a soirée.*

PHOTOGRAPHS FRENCH FILM OFFICE

Henry B. Darrach, an associate editor of Time, *regularly contemplates the world of cinema and its personalities as that magazine's film critic. He also contributes book reviews to* Time *and is himself a writer of fiction and poetry.*

55

IN SEARCH OF THE
ETRUSCANS

A GREAT PEOPLE STILL SHADOWED
IN MYSTERY EMERGE THROUGH THE
NEWEST TOOLS OF ARCHAEOLOGY

The Greeks and the Romans were scandalized by the privileged role women enjoyed in Etruscan society, even to reclining beside their husbands on the banquet couch. The handsome couple who grace the lid of this terra-cotta sarcophagus are commemorated while dining together. The sculpture is in the collection of the Museum of the Villa Giulia, Rome.

FROM *Etruscan Art*, SILVANA EDITORIALE D'ARTE

There is a queer stillness and a curious repose about the Etruscan places I have been to, quite different from the weirdness of Celtic places, the slightly repellent feeling of Rome and the old Campagna, and the rather horrible feeling of the great pyramid places in Mexico . . . or the amiably idolatrous Buddha places in Ceylon. There is a stillness and a softness in these great grassy mounds with their ancient stone girdles, and down the central walk there lingers still a kind of homeliness and happiness. True, it was a still and sunny afternoon in April, and larks rose from the soft grass of the tombs. But there was a stillness and a soothingness in all the air, in that sunken place, and a feeling that it was good for one's soul to be there.

D. H. Lawrence, Etruscan Places, *Viking Press*

IN SEARCH OF THE

ETRUSCANS

By RAYMOND BLOCH

For the traveler today, leaving the flat campagna on which Rome is situated and journeying north along the Via Aurelia, the old Roman road, it is as easy to evoke the shades of the Etruscans as it was for D. H. Lawrence some forty years ago. That sensitive and restless wanderer set out to see for himself the countryside that still bears the name of a near mythic race of hot-blooded people, and he was not disappointed. As one enters Tuscany the country grows more rugged, the road climbs and winds through hills dotted with the writhing cypresses and through fields lush with asphodel, the true Tuscan flower, with its vivid hue and earthy fragrance. Lawrence walked the dusty roads that led then, and still do, through the turf-covered mounds that mark the ancient cemeteries. And he marveled at the paintings with which the Etruscans decorated their tombs cut out of the volcanic rock, the *tufa*.

Created to solace the dead, these tomb paintings tell a rich and joyous story of Etruscan life and civilization. Here is Lawrence's description of the Tomb of the Leopards, which contains the painting reproduced on pages 68 and 69:

The walls of this little tomb are a dance of real delight. The room seems inhabited still by Etruscans of the sixth century before Christ, a vivid, life-accepting people, who must have lived with real fullness. . . .

The dancers on the right wall move with a strange, powerful alertness onwards. They are men dressed only in a loose coloured scarf, or in the gay handsome chlamys draped as a mantle. The subulo *plays the double flute the Etruscans loved so much, touching the stops with big, exaggerated hands, the man behind him touches the seven-stringed lyre, the man in front turns round and signals with his left hand, holding a big wine-bowl in his right. And so they move on, on their long, sandalled feet, past the little berried olive-trees, swiftly going with their limbs full of life, full of life to the tips.*

This sense of vigorous, strong-bodied liveliness is charac-

teristic of the Etruscans, and is somehow beyond art. You cannot think of art, but only of life itself, as if this were the very life of the Etruscans, dancing in their coloured wraps with massive yet exuberant naked limbs, ruddy from the air and the sea-light, dancing and fluting along through the little olive-trees, out in the fresh day.

Virtually all the wall painting of the classic world before the days of Imperial Rome has vanished, save that of the Etruscans. The tomb paintings are thus a unique treasure, although a wasting one. Many of the tombs were broken open centuries ago by looters who carried off all the movable treasure of gold and sculpture and jewelry. The frescoes that so delighted Lawrence remained, but they were flaking fast from the effects of air and moisture. No new tombs had been found for a generation, nor were any further ones to be found for a generation to come. Indeed, it is only within the last few years that a new method of archaeology has shone a tiny but powerful light into the secret places of the Etruscan past. It appears now that an unknown multitude of painted men and women may lie still hidden beneath the Tuscan soil.

The new burst of discovery in Etruscan tomb painting owes its origin not to a professional archaeologist but to an Italian industrialist named Carlo M. Lerici, for whom archaeology is a passion. Signor Lerici determined to prospect for tombs as a mining engineer prospects for ore. He equipped a team with potentiometers and electro-magnetic and seismic wave devices, such as engineers use to locate underground deposits, and a unique archaeological tool: a camera with a long periscope that could be lowered into holes bored in the ground. The study of aerial photographs made of Etruscan necropoli indicated the most suitable sites for investigation, and the refined electrical apparatus precisely located the center of tombs that remained sealed beneath the earth.

On the morning of March 26, 1958, in the necropolis at

A *new era in Etruscology has been opened by the application of tools originally designed for different uses. This aerial photograph, made originally for a tax survey in 1938, reveals the buried tombs in the Etruscan necropolis of Tarquinia. The hundreds of white marks represent the now leveled mounds that surmounted each sepulcher. These "soil marks" result from the mixing of earth with debris from the tomb.*

Tarquinia, Lerici's three-man team drilled a hole and let down their periscope. They were only moderately hopeful, for during the previous two months they had already opened eighty tombs in this necropolis, only to find them barren. But they rotated their periscope, permitting the camera, with its own light source, to make a series of photographs through 360 degrees around the tomb. Then they took the camera out and sealed the hole to prevent the entry of air, which could destroy any painting that might be within the tomb.

When the photographs were developed, the gratified Lerici could announce the first discovery of a painted Etruscan tomb since 1892. Because the scenes were of athletes in a contest (see page 63), it was named the Tomb of the Olympiad. The tomb has since been opened and the paintings removed by the Istituto del Restauro for eventual display in a museum, where they may be best preserved. Carlo Lerici and his staff have gone on to locate eight more painted tombs, and thus to open up a new era in Etruscology.

The common impression of the Etruscans is that they were a most mysterious people. Appearing in the heart of Italy during the eighth century before Christ, they developed a brilliant civilization there which flourished until almost the beginning of the Christian Era. And they came very close to achieving the unification of the peninsula with themselves as its overlords. As forerunners of Roman power, even in antiquity the Etruscans attracted the attention of Greek and Roman writers. As foes and, indeed, onetime rulers of Rome, the Etruscans were regarded by the Romans with respect, but this attitude was tinctured by disdain for their uninhibited and luxurious way of life, which the Romans thought decadent. Yet the Romans, ever admiring of other peoples' art, prized that of the Etruscans, and they collected their artifacts avidly.

So much is fact. Yet about the Etruscan civilization clings enigma, which no discoveries of art or inscription have been able to dispel. Where did these first masters of Tuscany come from? And what language did they speak?

For most of the ancient writers, the question of Etruscan

This strange figure is Carlo M. Lerici, the industrialist-engineer whose techniques have revolutionized Etruscan archaeology. Having drilled a shaft through the top of an unopened tomb, Signor Lerici examines it through a Nistri periscope. A camera with its own light source may then be attached to record the condition of the tomb and its contents. In this way, the color photograph on page 63 was obtained.

origin was already answered. They followed the account given by Herodotus, according to which the Etruscans had come to Italy from the shores of Asia Minor, more precisely from Lydia. As the first great Greek historian tells it in his lively style—and according to a very early chronology which is his own—the Lydian people suffered a devastating famine in the thirteenth century before our era. Since the nation's survival was imperiled, King Atys decided to send part of the population abroad. He divided the Lydians into two groups: one to remain at home under his rule, the other to emigrate under his son Tyrrhenus. The king's mandate was carried out and Tyrrhenus and his followers sailed from Smyrna. After a long voyage they reached the hospitable shores of western Italy. To the sea on whose shore they had settled, they gave the name Tyrrhenian, by which it is known to this day. In their own language they called themselves *Rasena*, while the Romans called them *Tusci* or *Etrusci*, terms which are still used to designate them and from which come the ancient and modern names of their province, Etruria and Tuscany.

The ancients unquestioningly accepted this tradition transmitted by Herodotus: Seneca wrote that Asia Minor claimed to have fathered the Tuscans. No one except Dionysius of Halicarnassus, a Greek rhetorician who lived in Rome in the days of Augustus, suggested any other solution. Since in his opinion the Etruscans resembled the Lydians neither in language nor religion nor customs, and he could discover no visible kinship between them and any known people, Dionysius concluded that they were a very ancient and indigenous people, born as it were from the soil they occupied.

These two theories—for an Oriental origin or an indigenous Italian one—held the field until the eighteenth century, when a French scholar, Nicolas Fréret, proposed a third solution. It was Fréret's opinion—still held by some scholars—that the Etruscans came from the north in one of the waves of Indo-European invaders that swept over Italy beginning in the second millennium B.C. But since this hypothesis has not one solid argument to support it, it may be

Some fruits of Signor Lerici's exploration are shown here. The photograph at right was made in 1958 by introducing into a still unopened tomb a source of light at the end of a periscope with a camera attached. It shows a section of the murals in the first painted tomb found since 1892, which its discoverers have named the Tomb of the Olympiad. Scholars believe that it was painted late in the sixth century B.C. Although this tomb overshadows their other finds because of the age and quality of its frescoes, Lerici's group has discovered eight other tombs containing paintings in good condition. At left is a photograph of one of them, the Tomb of the Red Lions. It was made shortly after the subterranean chamber was opened.

confidently rejected. So the choice remains between the original alternatives.

A considerable number of linguistic and archaeological facts buttress the argument that the Etruscan roots lie in Asia Minor. One is a discovery made at the end of the last century on the island of Lemnos in the Aegean Sea, close to the Asian coast. The discovery was that of a funerary stele with an inscription in a language that was unknown but obviously related to Etruscan. This document and a few similar inscriptions could be explained if the Tyrrhenians, journeying from Lydia, had stopped at Aegean islands such as Lemnos. Many aspects of the civilization of Etruria— social usages, religious beliefs, and artistic techniques—relate it to the Oriental world. For example, in Crete and certain ancient kingdoms of Asia Minor, women occupied a privileged place in society. Instead of living in seclusion as the Greek woman did, she was present at games, spectacles, and banquets. All evidence seems to indicate that the Etruscan woman played a role of similar importance in social life. Her position may thus represent a trace of an ancient matriarchy of Oriental type.

But it is probably the Etruscan religion that presents the greatest number of resemblances to Asiatic faiths. The Etruscan religion was a revealed religion; its precepts were contained in sacred books, and through the rather numerous indications left by Greek and Roman writers, we know the contents of these books. The Etruscans believed that Tages, a genius miraculously sprung from the earth, and a nymph named Begoe had imparted the code of rules which were to govern Etruscan religious life, as well as a whole series of precepts that represented a systematic explanation of life and death, of the world and its destiny. This formalism is fundamentally different from the hospitable and undogmatic polytheism of the Greeks and Romans.

The Etruscans worshiped gods grouped in triads, as was often the case in the world of Crete and Mycenae. They were constantly seeking to discover the will of the gods by subtle methods of analyzing signs, which they believed their divinities sent to them. Their priests, the haruspices, were masters of the art of divination, studying all manner of omens—thunder and lightning, monstrous births in the human and animal kingdoms. From these analyses they drew

detailed conclusions as to what course their people should pursue. Their favorite method of divination consisted in examining the livers of animal victims offered in sacrifice to the gods. Since the Tuscan divinities, who each occupied a particular region of the sky, likewise ruled over various areas of the livers of sacrificial victims, their intentions and commands could be read from the appearance of these organs. Behind this lies a peculiar conception of the world, a conception belonging to a still half-magical mentality, typical of Assyro-Babylonian countries.

This series of facts pointing in the same direction does not convince those who adhere to the theory of an indigenous origin for the Etruscans. These scholars recognize the connections between the Etruscan and Oriental peoples, but they believe that these can be explained by other means than migration. In their view, the ancient peoples who occupied the shores of the Mediterranean, and who were partly submerged by invaders from the north, left behind a certain number of ethnic nuclei, or "islands," as survivors of the general shipwreck. These continue to inhabit the places where they had settled in their remote past. The Etruscans,

then, would represent one of these nuclei, and this would account for their kinship with various ancient Oriental peoples who were related ethnic survivors. And had the Etruscan civilization developed from one of these ethnic nuclei, this would explain its Italic characteristics.

It is certainly difficult to decide a problem so complex. That the actual civilization of the ancient Tuscans developed on the spot is an unquestionable fact. And a mixture of various peoples indubitably went into the making of the Etruscans, for we cannot believe that the whole Etruscan people, as we know them, appeared on the Tyrrhenian littoral at some particular time. The question remains whether we should not retain the hypothesis of a partial migration of colonists from the extreme eastern Mediterranean, probably at the end of the eighth century B.C. Viewed in this way, such a migration seems highly plausible, as it accounts for a number of features in Etruscan life that would otherwise be difficult to understand.

There is another problem which the efforts of investigators have not yet succeeded in solving—the mystery of the Etruscan language. It remains one of the few languages that pose

63

insurmountable difficulties to scholars. To read and understand Etruscan with ease remains but a hope.

This is all the more curious since there is no lack of linguistic material. More than ten thousand inscriptions survive, found in Tuscany, Campania, and Latium, and engraved or painted on the most varied monuments and artifacts. It is true that the vast majority of these inscriptions are hopelessly short; for the most part funerary or votive texts, they usually do no more than enumerate the names of the dead person or the dedicator, together with his ancestry and age. Only a dozen texts run close to a hundred words. One manuscript text is somewhat longer, a linen book containing fifteen hundred words. This book has had a curious fate: during the Roman period it was cut into wrappings for an Alexandrian mummy, which in modern times was brought to the museum at Zagreb. This mummy-cloth book constitutes a basic document of Etruscological research.

To these direct sources, we must add the information concerning the Etruscan language supplied by certain Greek and Latin compilers, such as the Alexandrian Hesychius. Some thirty Etruscan words, translated by them, are known to us beyond any possibility of doubt.

All of these texts can be read without difficulty, for the Etruscan alphabet is of the Greek type, and may have been borrowed either from Greece, from the eastern Mediterranean basin, or from the people of the Greek city of Cumae near present-day Naples. To decipher the Tuscan alphabetical symbols and read Etruscan inscriptions is now an easy matter. Moreover, we have considerable knowledge of Etruscan grammar, whose phonetics are known to us from the Etruscan transcriptions of Greek mythological names found on a number of monuments. The qualities of the vowels often vary, and voiced consonants are absent. The tongue has a marked tendency to aspiration, and this phenomenon has rightly been compared with one of the most curious characteristics of the modern Tuscan idiom—the aspiration of guttural consonants in certain positions. For example, the Tuscans of today still call a house (*casa* in Italian) *hasa*. Linguists agree in regarding this phenomenon, which is exceptional in Italy, as a distant heritage from Etruscan phonetic tendencies.

Even the structure of Etruscan appears markedly different from that of the Indo-European languages. We know the declensions, but the verbs, little represented in the inscriptions, largely escape us. It is on the semantic plane that we are most at a loss. Despite the thousandfold attempts of investigators, barely a hundred verbal roots have been deciphered with certainty. These suffice, it is true, for an understanding of the shortest inscriptions identifying the donor or the deceased. But our uncertainty increases many times over in the case of longer texts, such as those of the Zagreb mummy-cloth book or the Capuan tile—a tile engraved with a long ritual message honoring the gods of the infernal regions. We can make out that they are documents describing the sacrifices to be performed on certain occasions, but the obscurities are overwhelming, and in the Capuan tile especially, whole passages remain completely dark.

This does not discourage research. One line of study attempts to illuminate still undeciphered words by comparing them with similar words which occur in other languages. But this etymological method, as it is called, is extremely dangerous, since no kinship has been established between Etruscan and any other language. The method known as "combinatory," or inductive, proceeds more wisely by studying Etruscan from within. Analogous Etruscan words or phrases are compared in the hope that those whose meanings are already known will lead to an understanding of the others. This requires great patience and nicety, and the results are often slight.

Recently scholars have tried comparing Etruscan texts that are still obscure—but whose religious nature can be divined—with Latin, Umbrian, and Oscan writings of the same nature. This really represents the creation of artificial bilingual texts, and the method is well justified because there were constant contacts among the peoples of central Italy and very probable resemblances between some of their religious rituals. Important results have already been obtained. However, the present impasse can undergo no radical change unless archaeologists discover some long bilingual text presenting an Etruscan composition and its translation into a known language—Latin or Oscan or Umbrian. Just as the Rosetta Stone was found, the expectation of finding some such Etruscan key is not unreasonable, and progress in archaeological methods justifies fresh hopes.

In contrast to these obscurities and mysteries, the actual life and civilization of the Etruscan people are brilliantly illuminated for us by the writings of the ancients and, above all, by the immense pictorial documentation of the tombs.

The beginning of the seventh century B.C. marks the known emergence of the Etruscan people in Italy (it is to archaeology that we owe this knowledge, for the texts are silent on the subject). Their coastal cities were the first to develop, succeeding the earlier Villanovan settlements of the Iron Age. From the earliest period of Etruscan history their prosperity developed with surprising rapidity. The evidence lies in the tombs hollowed out of the earth to duplicate for the dead the rooms of their dwellings while alive, and in which they were laid richly decked with delicate treasures of the goldsmith's art. The seventh and sixth centuries before our era were a period of wealth and power for Etruria. This rapid rise is doubtless explained by the early exploitation of the copper and iron mines that abound in northern Etruria, especially around Populonia. The mountains of slag that were left testify to the extent of Etruscan mining and refining enterprise.

This metallurgical activity gave the developing nation both durable weapons and, through barter, the possibility of importing products necessary to its subsistence and its art.

TEXT CONTINUED ON PAGE 73

64

A PORTFOLIO OF
ETRUSCAN PAINTING

These eight pages present major Etruscan works in fresco, selected from Raymond Bloch's
Etruscan Art, published by Silvana Editoriale d'Arte, Milan, and the New York Graphic Society.
Above, warriors holding shields (detail), circa 530 B.C., from the Temple of Hera at Cerveteri.

Since classic Greek painting—except for the marvels of painted vases—survives only in a few scattered fragments and in the memory of literary descriptions, all that remains of true polychrome painting before the age of Imperial Rome is to be found in the tombs of the Etruscans. Here is preserved a record of Italic life through some six centuries, showing not only the customs of this vigorous people but also the influences, both Greek and Roman, that first nourished then ultimately destroyed them. For candor and realism, there are virtually no parallels in all archaic art to the frescoes painted about 520 B.C. in the Tomb of Hunting and Fishing at Tarquinia. In the detail at right, four fishermen tend their nets in a painted boat riding a wine-dark sea. Above them birds wheel, while alongside a dolphin cuts the waves.

Music and merriment were natural expressions of the warm Etruscan temperament. Painted about 475 B.C., the above detail from a banquet scene, with a wine bearer leading a flutist and a lyre player, is remarkably well preserved in the Tomb of the Leopards at Tarquinia.

A ritual dance for the dead is depicted in the scene above from the Tomb of the Lionesses at Tarquinia. Painted about 520 B.C., the figures have stylistic forms suggestive of the archaic Greek, but their intense animation is typically Etruscan. The profile of a noble lady (opposite), identified by an inscription as Velia, was painted in the Tomb of Orcus at Tarquinia about 300 B.C. Her mien reflects by its dignified restraint the influence of the classic period. The badly damaged fresco of which her portrait is a part presents a feast; that it is laid in the nether world is indicated by the silhouetting black cloud.

TEXT CONTINUED FROM PAGE 64

Etruscan vases and bronzes have turned up in Greece, France, England, Spain, Africa, and Eastern countries. A large fleet ensured the security of the commercial connections maintained with the western and eastern Mediterranean basin. At the same time other hardy, seafaring peoples, the Phoenicians and the Greeks, were creating a large number of markets and depots to facilitate their commercial exchanges. The Greeks and the Phoenicians eventually challenged each other, and in this maritime duel the Etruscans sided with the Phoenicians of Carthage because the Greeks were a threat to Etruria not only from the north, with their cities in Provence, Nice, and Marseilles, but also from the south, with their territories in Campania and Sicily. The alliance between the Carthaginians and the Etruscans, begun in the earliest days of the nation in the seventh century B.C., was to endure through practically the entire period of Etruscan independence.

During the seventh and sixth centuries, Etruria dominated the Tyrrhenian Sea, and the fame of its power spread wide. At the end of this period the Etruscans began to expand by land. Finding themselves opposed only by peoples of an inferior civilization who belonged to the family of Italic peoples—in Latium the Latins, in Campania the Oscans, in the plain of the Po various uncohesive tribes—the Etruscans spread out. They had little difficulty in occupying Latium, a large part of the rich Campania district in the south, and the fertile valley of the Po in the north. A little farther, and the whole of Italy would have come under their hegemony. Had that happened, the whole history of the peninsula and the West would have been vastly different. At this time Rome itself came under the power of Etruscan tyrants from Tarquinia. The site of Rome had been occupied from about 750 B.C. by Latin and Sabine tribes, and a Latin-Sabine settlement had gradually developed on the hills surrounding the depression of the Forum. Its progress had been continuous

but rather slow until the beginning of the sixth century B.C., when Rome came into direct contact with Tuscan civilization. The situation then changed, and Livy's colorful pages depict this prosperous period of an Etruscanized Rome, sister to the Etruscan towns established a little farther northward at Cerveteri and Veii.

The political and social organization of the Etruscans is known to us only fragmentarily. In the beginning, the government of each of their cities was a monarchy, the ruler a priest-king, or *lucomon*, whose royal insignia were exactly like those of the Tarquin rulers of Rome—gold crown and ring, scepter, the fasces, the curule chair. So homogeneous was the nature of the Etruscan city-states that scholars often speak of the Etruscan empire, but despite sharing a common race and civilization, the Etruscan cities were never able to achieve a genuine political and military union. The ties that bound them were solely religious: every year delegates from the different cities journeyed to celebrate the Pan-Etruscan games at a national sanctuary, the *Fanum Voltumnae*, in the vicinity of Lake Bolsena.

The Etruscans were exceptionally gifted in industry, commerce, and the arts, but they were lacking in the fundamental qualities that promoted the destiny of Rome—tenacity, patience, ability to organize. Early in the fifth century, central Italy was shaken by a series of constitutional crises; almost everywhere in the Oscan, Umbrian, and Latin countries, monarchies were supplanted by oligarchic republics. The twelve cities scattered over Etruria from north to south were not excepted. Small bodies of aristocrats came to rule them, in place of sacred kings. The plebs, or working part of the population, included artisans, merchants (often foreigners, frequently Greeks), and slaves. In Etruria, unlike Greece and Rome, there was no gradual emancipation of plebeians eager to share the powers of the ruling classes. Social divisions remained strict to the end, and this was certainly a source of weakness for the Etruscan empire. This fact, together with the graver fact of political disunion, prevented Etruria from taking full advantage of its strength. The period of Etruscan greatness was soon followed by reverses and decadence.

At the beginning of the fifth century, the combined pressure of Greeks and Latins forced the Etruscans to withdraw from Rome and the whole of Latium. In 474 B.C., Greek ships defeated them heavily at Cumae. In the course of the next century they lost Campania to the Samnites, a warlike mountain people attracted by the wealth and the mild climate of the Campanian coast. The wars with Rome continued. While threatened from the south by the advancing Roman legions, the Tuscan cities had to defend themselves in the north against Celtic peoples from Central Europe, wandering in search of fertile soil. From the fifth century B.C., these warlike tribes repeatedly descended on the Italian peninsula, and the Romans themselves suffered disastrous defeats at their hands. The Etruscans put up a strong resistance but

ANCIENT WRITERS ON THE ETRUSCANS

The Tyrrhenians fight, knead dough and beat their slaves to the sound of the flute.

ARISTOTLE, quoted by Pollux, *Vocabulary*, IV, 56

We are told that the Tuscans not only catch deer and boars by means of nets and dogs, as is the normal custom in the field, but even more frequently by the aid of music. This is how they do it. On all sides they set out nets and other instruments of the chase to lay traps for the animals. A skilful flautist takes up position and plays the purest and most harmonious melody. He plays the sweetest airs the flute is capable of producing. When the sound comes to their ears, they are at first astonished and afraid, then they are overcome by the irresistible pleasure of the music and, transported, they forget their young and their lairs. Yet animals do not like to go far from their homes. Yet, as if drawn by some charm, they are forced to approach and the power of the melody makes them fall into the nets, the victims of music.

ÆLIAN, *On the Nature of Animals*, XII, 46

It remains for us now to speak of the Tyrrhenians. . . . the authors of that dignity which surrounds rulers, providing their rulers with lictors and an ivory stool and a toga with a purple band; and in connection with their houses they invented the peristyle, a useful device for avoiding the confusion connected with the attending throngs; and these things were adopted for the most part by the Romans, who added to their embellishment and transferred them to their own political institutions. Letters, and the teaching about Nature and the gods they also brought to greater perfection, and they elaborated the art of divination by thunder and lightning more than all other men.

. . . Twice each day they spread costly tables and upon them everything that is appropriate to excessive luxury, providing gay-coloured couches and having ready at hand a multitude of silver drinking-cups of every description and servants-in-waiting in no small number; and these attendants are some of them of exceeding comeliness and others are arrayed in clothing more costly than befits the station of a slave.

DIODORUS SICULUS, *Historical Library*, V, 40, Loeb Classical Library

Even the city of Volsinii was infested with vice and suffered a sad and direful catastrophe. It was rich, it was adorned with customs and laws; it was the head and metropolis of Etruria. But when once luxury crept in, it fell into an abyss of injury and infamy till it became subjected to the insolent power of her slaves who, at first in a small number daring to enter the Senate, in a short time overturned and mastered the whole Commonwealth. They ordered wills to be made at their own pleasure. They forbade meetings and feastings of freemen, and married the daughters of their former masters.

VALERIUS MAXIMUS, *Memorable Actions and Sayings*, IX, I

were forced to yield in the north. The valley of the Po passed to the hostile and turbulent Celts.

From the middle of the fourth century B.C., Etruscan power was only a memory. One after another, their cities fell before the assaults of the Romans, who were methodically proceeding to conquer the center of the peninsula. About 260 B.C., the last stronghold of Etruscan independence, Volsinii, some sixty miles north of Rome, succumbed to a merciless siege. Then, little by little, the whole of Tuscany became part of Roman Italy.

Artistic and religious traditions survived the loss of freedom, and until approximately the beginning of the Christian Era the workshops of the conquered province continued to produce large numbers of art objects in the distinctive local style. But even these vestiges of Etruscan civilization vanished during the devastation brought on by the civil wars between the armies of Marius and Sulla at the beginning of the first century B.C. Thereafter Etruria as a separate entity remained only as a field of study for lovers of the past.

That this past lives again before our eyes we owe to the Etruscan funeral monuments. The fate of the dead and the other world were constant concerns of the Etruscans. The idea of death weighed on them perpetually and terribly. The Etruscan tomb was built in the image of the Etruscan house so that the deceased within could lead after death a life that the Etruscans believed to be quite real, if diminished. Within the tombs men lay with their weapons, women with their jewelry. Animals were sacrificed to provide blood, and offerings of wine were placed near at hand so that the dead in their weakness might be nourished.

Except for the frescoes, the tombs are now bare of ornament or furnishing. But from them came the troves of sculpture, pottery, vases, mirrors, and jewelry which grace the museums of Italy and the world. Even Etruscan architecture is known almost wholly from the tombs, for excepting parts of imposing walls and gates, little is left of Etruscan cities above the ground. Houses and even temples in great part were built of perishable materials which time and the hands of men have caused to vanish. But the documentation of the

One of the highest accomplishments of the Etruscan artisan was the casting and engraving of bronze mirrors and vessels. Of the thousands of examples that survive, few equal in mastery or refinement this toilet box known as the Barberini casket, after the noble family that formerly possessed it. The finely incised scenes show Hermes standing before Paris and, to the right, galloping horses drawing a quadriga. On the lid, two Amazons bearing a dead comrade compose the handle; the feet of the casket are those of lions resting atop toads. The cannister, from the late fourth century B.C., is now in the Museum of the Villa Giulia, Rome.

Etruscan art received its chief inspiration from Greece, but its human figures, even when stylized, are seldom as idealized as their Greek prototypes. Perhaps because few of their gods —only those adopted from the Greeks—were endowed with human form, Etruscan artists conceived the body as less divine than did the Greeks. The subjects of Etruscan art are often human beings rather than gods or mythic heroes. The bronze figurine opposite, from the early fifth century B.C., only five and one half inches high, is characteristically Etruscan. Although it is slightly stylized, with swelling form and slender waist, after the Ionic mode, it is intensely animated, depicting an arrested moment of surely observed equipoise and suppleness. The statuette is in the Museum of Ancient Art, Munich. In the Civic Museum of Chiusi is the archaic bronze mask, above, from the first half of the seventh century B.C. It was originally attached to a burial urn and was meant to be a representation of the departed.

tombs, in their furnishings and mural scenes, presents us with an image of the homes of the living.

The world of Tuscan plastic arts is surprisingly rich and diversified. If stone sculpture in the round is seldom of high quality, the bas-reliefs in soft stone at Chiusi present admirable renderings of scenes from games and the dance. The imitation of Greek plastic art was a constant procedure in Tuscany, and as in the case of all Etruscan art, the Greek model can easily be discerned behind the Etruscan replica; but the Tuscan temperament delights in bold stylization and personal vision rather than in harmony of form. There is more pure beauty in Hellas, more expression of freedom in Etruria. Often the forms are greatly elongated, the draperies stylized to the extreme, and the action rendered in its momentary and intense dynamism. It is the man with his individual traits that interests the Etruscan artist; it is a particular face and particular characteristics that he is concerned with perpetuating. Late in its history, Etruscan portraiture produced a number of masterpieces. We do not know the names of the men whose striking visages have come down to us, but the fact that they are portraits is clear from their unmistakable individuality. Surely the Romans' brilliant accomplishment of biting realism in portrait sculpture must have been partly nourished from this Etruscan source.

There is one realm of art which, perhaps more than any other, restores to our vision the extraordinary virtuosity of the Etruscan artists. It is that of the goldsmith, which the most recent archaeological and linguistic researches indicate was brought from the Caucausus and the Aegean countries. The techniques of filigree and granulation made possible the reduction of gold to extremely fine threads or to tiny spheres, which enabled the goldsmith to decorate the surfaces of jewelry—bracelets, earrings, or necklaces—with infinite delicacy. The masterpieces of Tuscan goldsmiths' work remain unmatched and unmatchable even today. (Even in so small an object as the pendant of the river-god Achelous, on the cover of this issue, Etruscan goldsmiths could create works of striking power.)

Still it is to mural painting that we return for our most detailed and vivid picture of Etruscan civilization. The Tuscan art of fresco painting made use of preliminary drawings of figures and silhouettes which were sketched either on a coating or directly on the rock. Very simple colors were added to fill the surfaces so prepared. The outlining of contours and the quality of design are immediately striking, the coloring clear and lively, and the total effect is remarkable for charm and freshness. In all, about a hundred painted tombs have been discovered, most of them in the cities of Tarquinia, Orvieto, and Chiusi, where specialized workshops must have lingered on. But only some twenty of the tombs opened before this century contain frescoes that are still intact. All the other paintings have disappeared due to the harmful effects of atmospheric variation—much more destructive once the chambers have been opened—and to the

dampness of the rock walls. More than once the Istituto del Restauro at Rome has performed the delicate operation of transferring damaged frescoes to museums where they can be preserved from further harm.

The tomb paintings depict the occupations and pleasures of the deceased. Within these solemn crypts they reflect a life of gaiety, refinement, and luxury. Reclining side by side on banqueting couches, the men and women of the Tuscan aristocracy feast joyously, waited on zealously by a graceful throng of servitors. Around them the male and female dancers abandon themselves to rhythms measured out by citharas and flutes. Elsewhere, soldiers and athletes take part in a series of games such as were doubtless held at the funeral and were to be repeated in the other world. Still elsewhere, teams of horses trained for the utmost speed compete in hard-fought races. All this points to an easy, luxurious life; and it was in this softness and avidity for pleasure that the ancients believed they had found the deeper causes for the decline of the Etruscans.

Perhaps they were right. But for us the Etruscan taste for joyous life within a splendid setting has had one happy result: a pictorial record unmatched in classic art. The Etruscan murals bring to vivid life a people whose ways and origins were a mystery to the earliest Romans. They bear witness to a people who were in love with life and art and who, in the dwellings of their dead, have left inexhaustible testimony to their aspirations, their desires, and their joys.

Raymond Bloch, Professor of Latin Epigraphy and Roman Antiquities at the Sorbonne and author of three books on the Etruscans, has been studying their works in the field, near Bolsena in northern Latium. His article for Horizon *was translated by Willard R. Trask.*

The Etruscans executed little sculpture in stone, but they were masters in terra cotta. Among the greatest horses from the ancient world is this pair of winged steeds made about 300 B.C. Harnessed to the chariot of a god, they once adorned the pediment of a temple in the Etruscan city of Tarquinia (where they are today in the museum). They reveal an art no longer typically Etruscan, but one almost indistinguishable from the predominantly classic mode of Greece and Rome.

FROM Etruscan Art, SILVANA EDITORIALE D'ARTE

OUT OF A FAIR, A CITY

Victor Gruen proposes

a plan for a 1964 Fair that

could be converted into

a permanent community—

a full-scale demonstration

of what the city

of the future could be

One of the most memorable inventions of the nineteenth century—a period noted for innovations in every field of human endeavor—was the International World's Fair. More generally known by the properly pompous Victorian title of International Exposition of Art, Science, Industry, and Manufacture, it was a unique form of cross-world communication, celebrating equally the industrial revolution's advances in technology and the smug Victorian conviction that theirs was the best of all possible worlds. It provided an unparalleled record of man's progress and achievements and of the tastes of an adventurous age.

Today, however, the World's Fair is a tired institution. In spite of its brilliant past, it is a long time since it has startled the world with its products or offered stimulating or controversial ideas. No longer an instrument of genuine intellectual exchange, it has been reduced to an expeditious economic shot in the arm and an instrument of routine national propaganda. The projected New York World's Fair for 1964 promises to be more of the same. However, out of the nebulous dreams and politicians' proposals that have marked its birth has come one notable new idea, which, paradoxically, may never be realized at the Fair at all.

The project, which was first proposed last year for a Washington site by the architect and planner Victor Gruen and his associates, was rejected when Washington lost the Fair to New York. It is a design that includes every facet of a Fair's organization and construction, from its outlying approaches to its focal exhibits. But its most remarkable feature is that it is in effect a re-usable plan. For the Gruen plan would convert the fairgrounds and installations into a whole new satellite city after the Fair is over.

Not since Daniel H. Burnham laid out his "White City,"

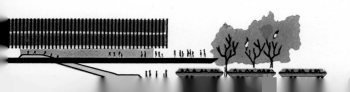

By ADA LOUISE HUXTABLE

for the Chicago Fair of 1893, has a scheme of comparable magnitude been proposed. Unlike Burnham's grandiose white plaster paean to the classic past, however, Gruen's design looks ahead. And while Burnham hoped to set an example with his monumental vistas and orderly avenues and arcades —later repeated in his master plan for Chicago—the Gruen proposal does even more: it blueprints a city for the future.

Nor is this proposal just a drawing-board dream. It is a diagram based on Gruen's practical experience ranging over twenty-five years in the fields of architecture, planning, and urban design. Probably no man in America today has a more intimate acquaintance with the ills of cities and their possible cures than he. Viennese by birth, Gruen came to this country in 1938 and has progressed from a one-man practice to his current position as head of a staff of two hundred, with principal offices in New York, Los Angeles, and Chicago. A small man with bold ideas, he combines solemnity, shrewdness, and a notoriously sharp wit. He is capable of leveling his opposition—for there is always opposition to the professional planner—with a few pertinent, devastating observations, delivered in a bland Viennese accent, with traditional Viennese charm. Gruen's office has produced some of the largest integrated architectural schemes in the country: the vast prototype shopping centers of Northland and Eastland, in Detroit, and Southdale, near Minneapolis. He is a specialist in the problems of the deteriorating and dying downtown centers of our older cities and the author of urban redevelopment projects for Fort Worth, Texas; Rochester, New York; Kalamazoo, Michigan; St. Paul, Minnesota; Fresno, California; and Paterson, New Jersey.

At the time when the proposal to hold a World's Fair in 1964 became serious, Gruen was called in by a group of

Washington businessmen representing the District's Board of Trade to prepare a study of an Exposition for the nation's capital. Los Angeles and New York were soon competing for the Fair, with New York pushing Washington hard. New York already had its old 1939 Fair site at Flushing Meadow, with some remaining facilities. The competing presentations were made to a three-man President's Commission charged with determining whether the United States should have a World's Fair in 1964 and, if so, where. Washington's ace was Gruen's plan, which he recommended for an area of open, rural land approximately ten miles east of the heart of the city, near Largo, Maryland. An architectural observer of the Washington scene, Frederick Gutheim, reported in the professional journal *Progressive Architecture*: ". . . while governors, mayors, ambassadors, and other talking dignitaries fell over themselves, each claiming the most for their proposition, it was architect Victor Gruen who carried off the palm. Other presentations raveled at the edges where promotional claims met the hard realities of land, time, or money; Gruen's neatly hemstitched article provided clear if admittedly preliminary answers. Unfortunately, the decision was not made on the basis of who was ready to produce what." The committee, subjected to rival pressure groups, was more impressed by New York's financial potential than by Gruen's plan. Although the decision put the Washington proposal into the realm of an unrealized dream, the Gruen scheme presents New York with a major challenge; for his plan offers a contribution of permanent value. It is a concept that promises comfort, convenience, and calculated visual pleasure instead of the customary catch-as-catch-can arrangement of commercial and national exhibits; and at the same time it provides the

This diagrammatic cross section shows a small part of the Gruen plan for a Fair. One of the raised platforms stretches across the center, while the end of another platform appears at left. Visitors arrive by train on the ground level and take escalators to the Fair buildings. Not shown in the cross section are footbridges connecting the platforms.

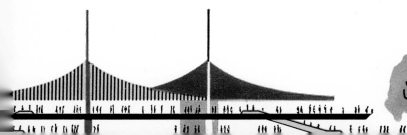

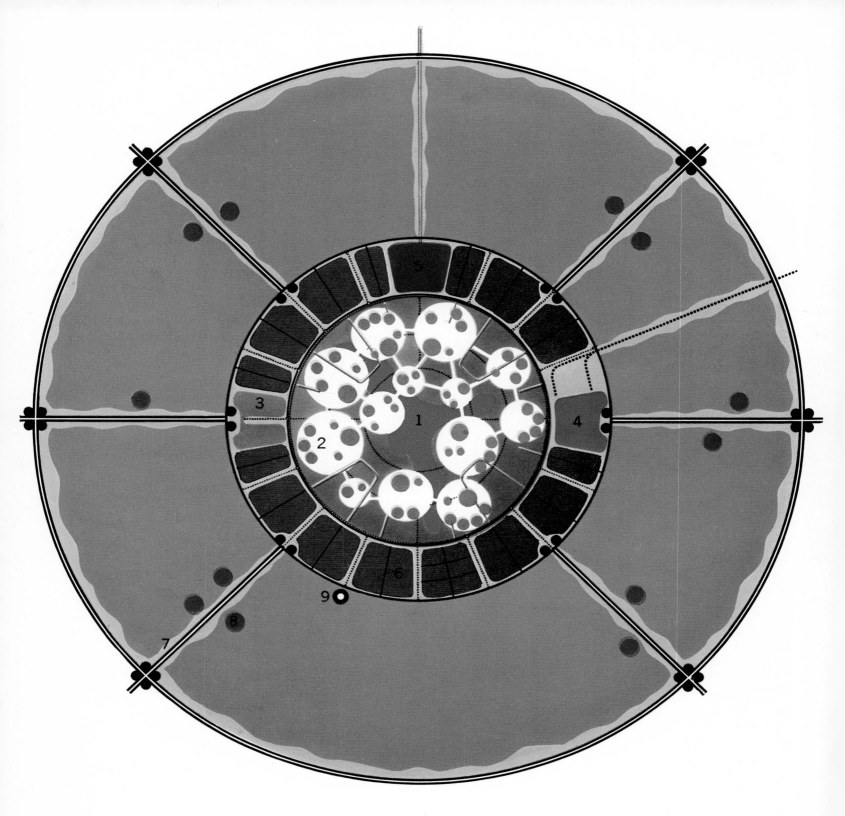

DURING THE FAIR

This is a diagrammatic visualization of the Gruen plan, designed to show the location, but not the shape, of areas and buildings. The shape of the Fair would be governed by the topography of the actual site, and the shapes of the buildings by their uses. All shades of green designate open areas. Large circles like (2) are the raised platforms carrying the Fair structures. Gray sections like (6) are parking areas for 100,000 cars. Heavy black lines like (7) are major arterial roads. Small circles like (8) are clusters of gas stations, motels, trailer parks, camping grounds, temporary housing, and other facilities. Broken black lines within the Fair area indicate intra-Fair passenger transit; red lines indicate intra-Fair freight and service transit. Others: (1) lagoon; (3) bus and taxi terminal; (4) rail and rapid transit terminal; (5) freight terminal; (9) heliport.

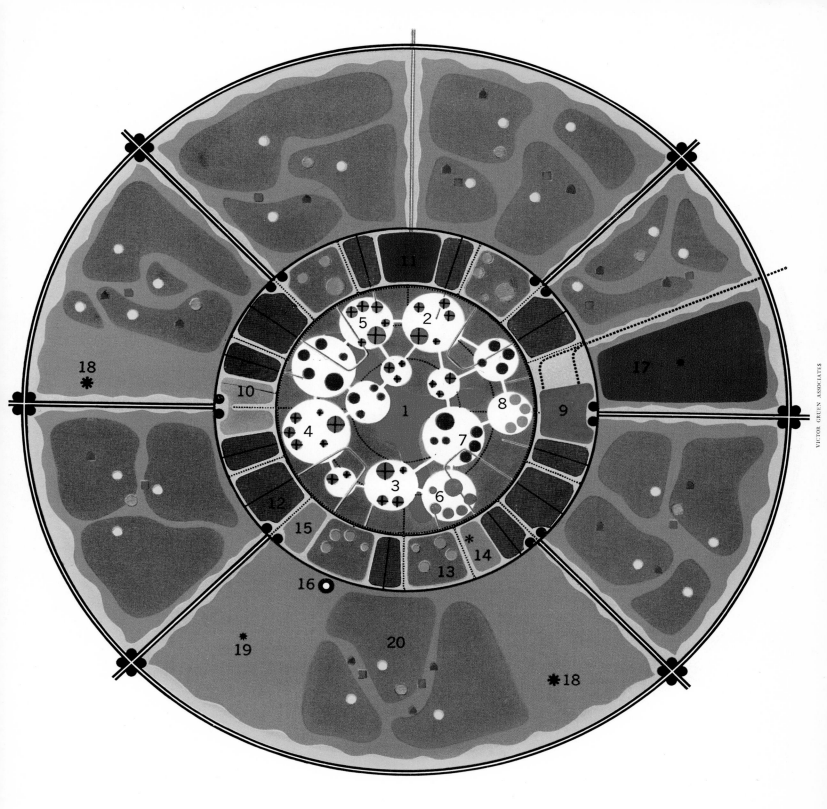

AFTER THE FAIR

This is a diagrammatic visualization of the city of 100,000 population which would be built on the Fair site. All shades of green indicate open areas. All heavy black lines indicate roads and transportation. (1) lagoon; (2) permanent trade center (converted); areas like (3) municipal and administrative offices (converted or retained); (4) amusement park (retained); (5) retail area (converted); (6) offices; areas like (7) high density residential; (8) medium density residential; (9) rail (10) bus (11) freight terminals; areas like (12) parking; areas like (13) medium density residential; (14) playground; (15) institutional and educational; (16) heliport; (17) industrial; (18) golf course; (19) playground; all complexes like (20) indicate residential areas including medium and low density housing, shopping centers, schools, churches, police and fire departments, motels.

Victor Gruen and associates

foundation for a well-designed community through the post-Fair employment of its existing layout, services, facilities, and even some of its buildings. Such a scheme supplies a proving ground for new approaches and ideas applicable to the solution of today's problems of rapid and scattered population expansion and the overwhelming specter of urban chaos and blight. As a practicing planner, Gruen welcomed the opportunity to put the latest and best theories into action. He realized immediately that the facilities needed to organize a modern Fair are equal to those required for a good-sized town; it was an obvious and logical step to plan an Exposition that could be effectively converted into a permanent community after the Fair had provided its six months of festivity and fun. The situation provided an unparalleled opportunity to avoid the familiar traps, pitfalls, and frustrations of uncontrolled, haphazard growth. "The new city will be a living expression of the plans and hopes of those deeply concerned with the disturbing manifesta-

This sketch of the Gruen plan during the Fair shows in left foreground a cutaway section of a raised platform, with service area beneath it. At center, a walkway leads from an internal transit stop to exhibition buildings and a terrace restaurant. In left background are the plastic-domed international shopping bazaar and footbridges connecting platforms. Right foreground contains the lagoon and a wooded picnic area.

tions of our urban crisis," said Gruen optimistically during his presentation to the President's Commission. "It will constitute a model city from which important lessons for planning and government can be derived." If the proposal failed to carry, the lessons are still there.

All of the familiar bugaboos of International Expositions have been anticipated and dealt with in this farsighted project. The question of traffic—the choking congestion that accompanies an influx of some 50,000,000 visitors to an urban or near-urban attraction—is solved by selecting a site sufficiently removed from the city and yet easily accessible by special roads that circumvent the city and its main arteries.

The usual temporary housing—stopgap measures that are taken to meet the jamming of facilities during Fairs, such as the jerry-built motor slums thrown up at the outskirts of Brussels in 1959—would be greatly reduced. Accommodations would be preplanned in part as permanent motels, hotels, and future housing for the new community that

would be expected to have an eventual population of 100,000.

The tragic and wasteful destruction that follows a Fair —in which good and bad architecture is torn down with equal, indiscriminating ruthlessness—would be avoided because the major structures would be retained for future civic use. (In addition, the town arising from the Washington Fair was to include a government-sponsored, permanent International Trade and Development Center, utilizing some exhibition buildings, and a National Recreation and Amusement Center that was to be derived from the entertainment sector of the Fair.)

The schematic diagram on page 82 of the model Fair shows a cluster of buildings on platforms, in a park. This is surrounded by parking and transportation facilities, ringed, in turn, by an outer area of open land. (The diagram uses symbolic circles; actually the elements would take on irregular shapes to conform to the site and topographical conditions.) The total area covered by the plan is 6,000 acres,

After the Fair the raised platforms remain, with service areas beneath them. The escalator and covered, air-conditioned walkway now lead to an apartment building in foreground, surrounded by new landscaping. Offices on platform in right background replace exhibition buildings. The domed international bazaar at left becomes the main shopping center. The lagoon for water sports remains the center for recreation.

85

based on 600 acres of exhibition ground, 900 acres of transportation facilities, and a surrounding 4,500 acres of "controlled environment."

Such a surrounding environment has never been part of a Fair plan before. The purpose of such an all-inclusive plan, according to Gruen, is to distribute traffic flow efficiently and to provide an attractive, planned approach. He declares that "We want to avoid the slumlike, shanty-town developments which have been typical of past Fairs and which consisted of an unattractive and typical mixture of gas stations, private parking lots, temporary eating facilities, emergency housing, and posters and billboards." The visitor would approach the Fair through what Gruen calls "a well-organized environment." In the diagram, this outer area is represented by a green ring of 4,500 fringe acres, with major roads passing through. Between these roads are clusters of buildings and facilities—service stations, trailer parks, car rental establishments, private airfields, motels, camping grounds, and temporary housing—arranged for orderly distribution and easy accessibility by feeder roads. Then comes the narrow inner ring of the transportation area, which encloses the exhibition area at the center, with its pattern of connected platforms.

The feature that strikes the viewer most forcibly as he studies the plan, and one that would be even more remarkable in reality, is the orderly separation of pedestrian and vehicular traffic instead of the usual mélange of people and cars. This is an immediate demonstration of one of the most revolutionary tenets of modern planning philosophy: the need for complete division of various modes of traffic from one another and for separation of pedestrians from them all. It is the planner's belief that the automobile is a mixed blessing that causes as much distress as delight. Its conveniences are sharply offset by the problems of urban paralysis that it creates. To Gruen and other professionals, the life, liberty, and salvation of the city depend on its rigid control.

Assuming that the visitor were to approach by automobile through the countryside, he would leave his car in one of the parking lots in the transportation ring at the edge of the Fair. If he came by bus, train, taxi, or public transport, he would arrive in the same area. There is even a heliport to act as a "branch line" from the nearest airfield. A freight terminal, also located within the ring, would handle all trucking operations and freight service. From this point an internal transportation system would take over, with separate lines for people and goods. Quickly and easily the visitor would be whisked from parking lots or terminals to the exhibition area.

Completely free of vehicular traffic, the Fair itself consists of a series of raised platforms in a landscaped setting, as indicated by the connected circles on the diagram. On these platforms are pavilions and exhibition buildings grouped according to purpose or theme. The visitor would ascend to these buildings by escalator from the lower level of the platforms. The lower levels themselves would accommodate all internal traffic and working functions, such as heating and air conditioning plants, storage and workshops—utilities and services that would take up at least 200 more acres in a less compact plan. The exhibition platforms themselves would be a pedestrian preserve; no wheeled vehicles are necessary, for all is designed within easy walking distance. Connected by footbridges, the platforms are placed in a green park containing benches, sculpture, fountains, and a central lagoon that is also a setting for water shows and marine exhibits. The platforms and pavilions would be treated in varying ways, with changes in color, lighting, and landscaping for design variety.

Most interesting of all in the plan, however, is the subsequent metamorphosis of Fair into city, a neatly calculated trick of planning legerdemain. At first glance, "after" in the diagram on page 83 does not look much different from "before." But closer scrutiny shows the important transformation: although the basic elements remain, certain significant changes have been made. The fairgrounds are now the downtown area of the new city. The raised platforms, the inner circulation system, all utilities, air conditioning and heating systems, parks, lagoons, sculpture, and fountains stay on to serve and beautify the new city core. Structures like the Fair's administration and reception buildings would become the new city hall and convention center. The theaters, amusement park, concert hall, and hospital all remain. The Fair's international bazaar becomes a downtown retail area.

Burnham's "White City" for the 1893 Chicago Fair was laid out in wide avenues on a grand scale, but unlike Gruen's proposal, the architecture was classic and rooted in the past.

Within the downtown sector some locations would be converted to commercial uses or high density apartments. Public transport, freight, and parking facilities within the transportation ring would be retained to serve the city, with some of the former parking area redeveloped for medium density housing. The outer fringe area, already the site of motels, services, and some housing, would provide open land for additional low and medium density housing, schools, shopping centers, and civic services. It would also accommodate light industry, research plants, and laboratories. Provisions are indicated for golf courses, playgrounds, and regional parks.

The development of the new city, of course, would be spread over a considerable length of time, but all of the Fair planning would be directed toward the dual-purpose land usage that would make it a practical reality. All told, permanence would be achieved on three counts: the establishment of the new satellite city itself, the retention of an amusement park, and the facilities for a continuing exposition center.

Since World's Fairs are known to be deficit operations, permanence would also greatly aid Fair finances. The total estimated cost of a World's Fair today, arrived at in Gruen's study on the basis of previous experience with large shopping centers and urban planning, is approximately $529,000,000. About $390,000,000 of this would be carried by exhibitors and concessionaires, with the remaining $139,000,000 borne by the Fair corporation. But with the conversion to permanent use of existing services and facilities such as roads, utilities, public transportation, and some buildings, some $88,000,000 of the cost would represent recoverable assets. This, according to Gruen's figures, would leave a greatly reduced deficit of just over $50,000,000.

Although Gruen's plan was mapped specifically for Washington, its unusual features are proving of wide interest. It is a scheme that would be applicable for any city where sufficient open land is available, and its expert attack on modern planning problems is a challenge to municipal governments everywhere and to New York in particular. Only by producing a scheme as good as Gruen's can New York hope to live up to the record of earlier Fairs. It is a formidable tradition, for the achievements of the nineteenth-century International Expositions were unique. In art, architecture, industry, and culture, they were the common exchange ground of all that was interesting and new. Intensely competitive, each successive exhibition attempted to cap its predecessors in the daring of its progressive constructions and the magnificence of its artistic displays. As industry leaped forward, its advances were proudly advertised, and the world came to see and learn. If industry frequently outran art, the Fairs still were the showcase of all the important technical and aesthetic experiments of the age. Today, the mementos of their prestige are collectors' curios, but the most important souvenir of the World's Fair was ideas.

In recent years we have done less well. The traditional exchange of ideas has been replaced by ideological competitions and salesmen's superconventions. The Gruen plan, by offering a significant advance in Fair design, casts serious doubts on recent Fair practices. It raises particular issues as to the serviceability of New York's Flushing Meadow location, site of the Exposition in 1939, when far fewer people and automobiles were involved than would be today. There are, however, other locations in the New York area to which the plan might be adapted. Although it leaves certain important questions unanswered, such as how to deal with the many unpredictable factors of future community development, it provides a loose master framework that would make it possible to handle these factors with maximum efficiency and logic, as they arose. If New York's 1964 Fair is to bring pleasure as well as profit, we might remember Daniel H. Burnham's words for Chicago, "Let us make no little plans." For the desirability of a well-designed total environment is not to be underestimated. New Yorkers, who are becoming increasingly victimized by their urban problems, anticipate plans for their 1964 Fair with understandable trepidation. If this is to be the best of all possible Fairs, in the best of all possible worlds (to borrow a bit of Victorian optimism), the ideas of Gruen's plan might well be applied.

Ada Louise Huxtable, a contributing editor of Progressive Architecture *and author of the study* Pier Luigi Nervi, *wrote about "Street Furniture" in the November, 1959,* HORIZON.

The first World's Fair took place in London in 1851. The Crystal Palace (above), which housed its exhibits, was a revolutionary building of glass and iron in prefabricated sections.

Since prehistoric times

men have prized it,

risked their lives for it,

used it in art

and sometimes in magic—

yet it is a fragile substance

that readily

warps, cracks, breaks

A PASSION FOR IVORY

By IVAN T. SANDERSON

Man, with his infinite ingenuity, has made use of just about every substance on or below the surface of the earth. The vast majority of all these materials may be classed among a few great groups, like gems, or metals, or woods. But there are a few very odd and unique materials which long ago acquired a special position in man's economy or esteem. The most outstanding among them is the substance we loosely call ivory.

This material is unique in more than one way. First, while it is intrinsically a single substance, forming a little class of its own, it can have several possible origins. Then, it is comparatively rare—and it is costly, time-consuming, and almost invariably dangerous to procure. But its uniqueness has little to do with these considerations. Rather, it is due to the fact that it has always, apparently, held outstanding aesthetic appeal for all men. It is a material more precious than many of the baser gem stones and all metals but gold and

Ivory at its source: the tusks of the male African elephant, shown here, are larger but the female's are of finer quality.

platinum, and it has always been in some respects holy. This is really all very mysterious.

Since earliest times, ivory appears to have been the particular delight of the sculptor. Across Europe, Asia, and North Africa, in the rubbish of caves inhabited by paleolithic man after the last retreat of the northern ice, pieces of ivory can be found incised in patterns or carved into little figures. There are ivory implements like needles and crude combs, and ivory statuettes with facial and bodily features clearly indicative of what are called the proto-Negroes, whose descendants we know today as the Bushmen of South Africa. All the early cultures, with the exception of the Sumerian, collected ivory and made both practical and artistic use of it. Two millennia before the birth of Christ there were wealthy collectors of ivories.

At the end of the fifteenth century, the Arabs had the ivory and slave trades, most intercontinental transport, and several other world enterprises firmly in their hands. When the Christian Europeans arrived upon the scene, the Arabs lost out because they were unable to compete, first, with the

According to this illustration from a book published in Antwerp about 1578, "Cave men in ambush cleverly hide from the elephants, seize their tails, then weaken them by attacking their knees." Some African hunters did capture elephants by hamstringing them, but the notion that a man could perch on an elephant's hind leg—which is quite straight—is as fanciful as the beasts' Mephistophelean ears.

new navigational aids devised by Henry of Portugal and, second, with the goods now issuing from the colonies of the New World. Port by port, tribe by tribe, and kingdom by kingdom, Islam had to retreat before the expanding West; the economy of the Orient, previously the hub of the universe, crumbled and fell into the hands of Europeans.

The Portuguese were the first to learn, as the Arabs had before them, that if they wanted anything out of Africa, they had to trade with the natives. Later the Spaniards, the Hollanders, the French, and finally the British learned that if they wanted slaves, they had to buy them from the African chieftains and princelings. And so it was with ivory. There were no elephants down on the coast, and even if one went into the forest one seldom saw them. Only by penetrating to the open savannas could one encounter them, but there the tribesmen were rather formidable. The extreme southern end of the continent was the only place where foreigners were able to amble inland and meet the African elephant. And that is just what the Hollanders did. Elsewhere, Europeans had to be content to trade with the natives or barter with Arabs who had already traded with the natives.

Although most Africans had not originally placed any particular value on ivory, they had found it just as satisfactory for carving and somewhat more durable than most of the harder woods. Since it came in fair-sized and gently curving pieces, they used it for making door lintels, stockades, and fences for graves. Moreover, elephants were good "beef"— one of them fed a lot of people—and their tough skins made good shields. They therefore hunted them as and when they could, and the chiefs made a habit of piling up the tusks be-

hind their houses as they were brought in by the hunters.

For many centuries the peoples that did value ivory—the Nubians, the Ethiopians, and the Arabs—had been able to satisfy their needs by trading for it around the upper Nile, and there had been no necessity for them to penetrate inner Africa. Thus, when the Europeans arrived on the coast, there was a monumental store of old ivory piled up all over equatorial Africa. Along with the incentive to collect ivory, the Europeans also brought new weapons—guns—far more efficient than the tribesmen's primitive spears and poisoned arrows. Together, white and black slaughtered the elephants wholesale until ivory flowed out of Africa in unbelievable quantity.

So wild was Africa that until the end of the last century only a few trade routes led into the heart of the continent. Apart from the short routes to the coast from inland Guinea, the only outlets from Central Africa were via the Congo, southeast via the Zambezi, directly east across what is now Tanganyika to Zanzibar, southeast from Uganda to Mombasa, or northeast via the upper Nile. When the Portuguese arrived, the Arabs controlled the last four routes, as they had controlled the whole east coast for centuries, and they were not disposed to give up their holdings. The Europeans might take ivory from the west coast—the Arabs could not prevent that—but on the east coast they had to buy it from them. And when the Europeans sailed round *behind* the Arabs, as it were, and cut off their other sources of supply in the Far East, it drove them back into Africa on a rampage that lasted two centuries. As late as 1888, Stanley could still say, bitterly, "Every pound weight [of ivory] has cost the life

of a man, woman, or child; for every five pounds a hut has been burned; for every two tusks a whole village has been destroyed; every twenty tusks have been obtained at the price of a district with all its people, villages, and plantations."

This violent scramble for ivory is inexplicable. Gems are pretty, portable, and rare, gold does not tarnish and is heavy, uranium is now very useful; but ivory cracks, warps, changes color, is eaten by rats, and breaks easily. Yet it has intrigued men throughout the ages. People who did not really know what it was placed a high value on it; and even now, long after the discovery of dozens of other substances that do equally well everything it does, people still pay a high price for it.

This regard for ivory may be partly mystical and may have originated in early Stone-age times, when objects made from it (notably sculptures in the round) seem to have acquired a religious connotation. Ivory, whether elephant, hippopotamus, walrus, sperm whale, or even narwhal or wild boar, was derived from the biggest and most impressive local animals. As the material from which teeth are made, it seemed alive; early man suffered from toothaches just as we do, and he knew only too well that human teeth grow and die. But teeth, as the least destructible parts of an animal, are its ultimate weapon. When a wondrous, powerful animal died, you might wear its teeth around your neck not only because they were pretty and durable, but because, not yet being wholly dead, they might retain some of the strength and power of the animal. One result is that, at various times and in many places, teeth came to be used as currency: the mighty hunter had many such teeth, for which lesser folk would trade all manner of things in the hope of acquiring some of his valor. In addition, ivory has always been a symbol of ecclesiastical prestige: the throne of the pope was once made of narwhal and elephant ivory. Today, the Elks cherish their ivory symbol of an elk's tooth.

The word "ivory" means several things. Derived from the stem *ebur*, its first and more basic meaning is simply "a heavy substance." In this respect it came to denote any hard white animal product, including the dense part of large bones and the homogeneous parts of any animal teeth, particularly their dentine and enamel. "Ivory" has also been used to mean the dried meat of the nuts of a South American plant known as the tagua (*Phytelephas macrocarpa*), which is indigenous to the hot tropical valleys leading down from the Andes. And the strange inorganic substance known as meerschaum, from which pipe bowls are carved, has often been called ivory, too. (Found on Arctic beaches and mined in Asia Minor, meerschaum is actually a hydrous magnesium silicate, called sepiolite.) But for us, the word "ivory" is restricted to the incisor teeth, or tusks, of the Asian and African elephants, mammoths, and—in exceptional cases—a few other extinct forms of elephants.

Prehistoric and ancient man worked for the most part in true ivory, but a very high proportion of ancient Egyptian ivory artifacts were made from the front teeth and tushes of the hippopotamus; these, although obviously smaller than elephant tusks, are finer grained, harder, and more durable. The outstanding ivory carvers of the ancient world were the Phoenicians. In fact, most of the raw ivory was handled by them; and most of the art objects collected by wealthy Egyptians, Assyrians, Babylonians, and Greeks were made

91

Some of the uses—religious, decorative, or utilitarian—to which ivory has been put (from left): Chinese figure of the Ming Dynasty (1368–1644), representing Shou-lao, the god of longevity, holding a peach; one leaf of a fifth-century diptych, or wax-filled writing tablet, showing a Roman consul sitting in his loge at the circus; two bishop's crosiers, a fourteenth-century Italian one at the left and a thirteenth-century German one at the right; an early sixteenth-century Benin mask from Nigeria, most likely worn as a breast plate; and a baleful-looking Afro-Portuguese object that may have been used—because of its slightly rounded base—for crushing peppercorns.

by them. The Phoenicians were seafarers and had a flourishing whaling industry based, it would appear, upon the sperm whale and the common dolphin. They did a brisk trade in the small teeth of the common dolphin, which commanded an extraordinary price in Persia both as ornaments and as charms. The Phoenicians also preferred the huge teeth of the sperm whale to those of any other animal, elephants not excluded, for carving their choicest ivories.

Ivory was also obtained from the larger kinds of wild hogs, such as the wart hog, and this is still in some demand in Germany where the tushes, having just the right curve, are used as handles for beer steins. In the far north, both in the Atlantic and the Pacific, two other kinds of ivory have been prized since before the dawn of history. These are the tusks of the walrus and the strange, spirally twisted "horns" of the narwhal. The narwhal is a small whale, the males of which have one or two such structures sticking straight out of their heads, sometimes to a length of twelve feet. Walrus ivory is very dense and pure, and although individual tusks seldom surpass twenty-four inches in length, all manner of artifacts and art objects have been made from it. In the Orient it went mostly to China, where it was used in the making of armor. The narwhal horns, though used for many such prac-

FROM LEFT TO RIGHT: COURTESY SPINK AND SON, LTD., LONDON; MUSEO CRISTIANO, BRESCIA; STIFTSAMMLUNGEN, KLOSTERNEUBURG; STIFT NONNBERG, SALZBURG; MUSEUM OF PRIMITIVE ART, NEW YORK; BRITISH MUSEUM, FROM *Afro-Portuguese Ivories*, BATCHWORTH PRESS, LTD.

tical things as sword handles, early acquired a religious connotation. They were marketed as the horns of unicorns, the kind shown protruding from the foreheads of rampant horses on the British coat of arms; and the Church in the West used them as legs and struts for episcopal thrones.

Elephant ivory comes in innumerable colors, consistencies, forms, and conditions. That of female African elephants is the finest. Yellowish and oily when first cut, it dries out to a pure white (the best grade is almost transparent, with a bluish cast). The best quality ivory from the Asiatic elephant starts out pure white but deteriorates with time to yellow, and eventually to dark brown. Mammoth ivory, being dead and very ancient, is friable and mostly full of cracks. But it is scattered all over northern Siberia and Alaska, and hundreds of thousands of tons have been dug up and exported over the centuries to both the Orient and the West (until it mysteriously disappeared from the Moscow market in 1934). Some mammoth ivory, however, is as pure, white, and dense as that of any contemporary elephant. But not all ivory is white or yellow. Almost all elephant ivory, while still borne by its rightful owners in the wild, has a thick brown overcoating, called "bark," which must be scraped off to disclose its true color. The tusk inside may be any shade of yellow,

olive, brown, mauve, or even jet black. Sometimes it may be naturally mottled. The tusks of both African and Asian elephants also vary enormously in shape and size. Both sexes of both species of African elephants, or loxodonts, bear tusks, but those of the males are larger. The bush loxodont has the larger tusks, but those of the forest loxodont often are much larger in proportion to the size of their bearers; furthermore, the longest forest loxodont tusks are much longer, though slimmer, than those of the bush species. The tusks of Asian elephants are much smaller and lighter than those of the African and are borne only by the males; those of the females, if developed at all, just reach the overfold of the lips and are barely visible. Strangely, today, the elephants of Ceylon are almost entirely tuskless, although it is recorded that they once bore tusks like their mainland relatives. There are also all manner of natural oddities occasionally met with.

Perhaps the oddest is known in Burma as *kyan zit,* in which both tusks are regularly ringed, constricted, and ridged throughout their length right up to their roots, like a bamboo. Another form resembles a corkscrew, which in extreme cases forms such a compact twist that the tusk is almost straight and bears a "thread" like the narwhal's spear or the tusks of the extinct South American elephant known

93

as *Cordillerion*. Both Asian and African elephants may be born with only one tusk or none at all, and three- and even four-tuskers have been found.

Ivory is highly elastic but as strong as spring steel, and a riding crop made from a lengthwise strip of it is as supple as a willow switch. Cut to the thickness of common typing paper, it is so transparent that standard print can be read through it; at the same time, its structure of concentric rings and small lozenge-shaped whorls, which look like the engine-turning on the back of a watch, becomes visible. Ivory is dentine, from which our own teeth are in large part made. It is "solidified" with phosphate of lime and other minerals including fluoride of calcium (the chief ingredient of tooth enamel), the percentage of which gradually increases in dead ivory to as much as 10 per cent. At the same time the gelatinous component gradually dries out, so that very old ivories tend to crumble (ancient ivory statues are restored by boiling in albumen or gelatin). Hippo and walrus teeth are covered with an immensely hard, flintlike dentine that will strike sparks from iron. It can hardly be cut and blunts files of the hardest tempered steel.

The finest ivory comes from West Africa between 10 degrees north and 10 degrees south of the equator. Some believe that the nearer to the equator, the better the ivory —but a glance at the map will show that these latitudes exactly enclose the range of the forest loxodont, from Gambia to Ruwenzori, and it is the ivory of that species which is the finest. The average size of tusks brought to the market today (which is still in London for "soft" ivory and in Amsterdam for "hard") is about fifty pounds in weight and from five to six feet in length. This ivory is almost all from African elephants; Asian elephants have not been hunted for some time for their ivory, and very little ivory now comes from the Orient.

The amount of ivory coming on the market today remains about the same from year to year, and its average price is about three dollars per pound. Prices in the past are hard to calculate. Each year about ten tons of ivory reach the market, which—at twenty elephants a ton—means only some two hundred elephants killed. However, a lot of "dead" or hoarded ivory still reaches the market. In addition, there are also the trophies carried away by modern licensed hunters and tourists. A considerable amount is used in Africa today by native and oriental craftsmen. Much of this is illegally poached. In 1893 more than sixty tons valued at £62,391 reached London from the Orient, and one hundred and fifty tons valued at £142,078 came from Africa. In other words, the price has a little more than doubled. During the period from 1870 to 1881, more than five thousand tons were imported into England. Going backwards still further, we find only forty tons imported in 1850, twenty-five in 1848, and fifteen in 1827. Thus, we are more or less back where we started when the great invasion of Africa and the ruthless slaughter of the loxodonts began.

A rather curious feature is the number of tusks that contain bullets, shot, or even spearheads embedded in them. The number would seem to be quite disproportionate, were it not that the average hunter aims for a headshot and the tusks begin far up in the head near the best point at which to aim. A bullet hitting a tusk will shatter it, but one penetrating the pulp cavity at its head will lodge there and slowly sink down into the pulp, eventually to be enveloped in the new ivory that grows outward layer by layer.

Ivory is cut with very thin circular saws that have to be whetted constantly. For very delicate operations it may even have to be cut under water (oil is seldom used because it is absorbed and stains the finished product). It is also, of course, sawed by hand and cut and carved with everything from a machete to a dentist's drill. Every scrap of the tusk is used. From the points, which are generally more solid and of finer grain than the rest of the tusk, come billiard balls, chessmen, and other hard-used utilitarian objects. The main shaft is delaminated and the plates used for such items as the handles of cutlery. In fact, this was once ivory's commonest use, and at one time a quarter of it went to Sheffield, England, for that purpose. Another quarter went to the towns of Ivoryton and Deep River in Connecticut and to a few other American cities where the keyboards of pianos were made. The scraps went, and still go, to button manufacturers. The sawdust is used as fertilizer, or is boiled down to make gelatin or a light sizing for straw hats and lace.

It has always been in the arts, however, that ivory has figured most prominently. We have already alluded to the ivories of the ancients, but we have not discussed the utterly amazing art of the Chinese—who still remain, after some four thousand years, the supreme ivory carvers. Their genius has for the most part been displayed in miniature: exquisite statuettes, models of temples and pagodas, animal statuary, and those mysterious series of carved hollow spheres, one within the other, that take years to execute but only a few dollars to purchase. Incidentally, I recall a gift given my

CONTINUED ON PAGE 120

Against the sheen of gilt and the rich colors of champlevé *enamel, the ivory figures of the Eltenberg reliquary still glow with undiminished luster after seven hundred years. Now in London's Victoria and Albert Museum, this reliquary was made for a Benedictine nunnery on the lower Rhine sometime during the second half of the twelfth century. It is in the shape of a small Byzantine church— Greek cross surmounted by a dome. The sculpture is all of walrus ivory: Christ and the eleven faithful Apostles seated above, sixteen prophets and four scenes from His life set in the niches below.*

94

Of all the exuberant and dynamic characters who crossed the stage of eighteenth-century England, few made a deeper impression than Charles James Fox—the subject of Karl Anton Hickel's somewhat disheveled portrait opposite. Because he was an unabashed rake, gambler, and wit, Victorian moralists found him easy game; even his contemporaries deplored his dissipations. But Fox was both a man of the world and a man of sense and feeling: a dedicated parliamentarian, student of poetry, and champion of advanced causes. For thirty-seven years a member of the House, several times a Cabinet member, and regularly the scourge of Tory prime ministers, it was he who struck the first blow for the abolition of the slave trade; and during their struggle for independence, the American colonists had no more zealous friend abroad.

The Rampant Fox

Because his public principles were as high as his private morals were low,

Americans benefited from this brilliant English Whig

Children who have been systematically spoiled are not always happy in their later lives. To be the offspring of a famous and successful man is sometimes a very grave drawback; and Henry Fox, the father of Charles James Fox, was both a famous and a doting parent, who had held high office, amassed a gigantic fortune, and, until he died, remained deeply devoted to his gifted, headstrong, spendthrift son. The process of spoiling the boy began in early childhood. Since Stephen, his elder brother, was a sickly child, plagued by a "distemper they call Sanvitoss dance," it was perfectly natural that Charles should have become the focus of all his father's hopes and schemes; but Henry Fox watched over his development as if he had been cultivating a rare and precious plant, which the smallest touch of neglect might cause to shrivel up and disappear. When his mother complained that Charles was "dreadfully passionate" and wondered what she ought to do, the great financier replied, "Oh, never mind; he is a very sensible little boy, and will learn to curb himself." Any form of contradiction, he felt, might inflict a serious mental injury: "Let nothing be done to break his spirit. The world will do that business fast enough."

Charles's spirit, however, proved quite indomitable; and, even as a baby, he seems to have taken full advantage of his anxious parent's good nature. Suppose that he wished to smash an expensive timepiece or plunge his sturdy arms into a bowl of cream: "Well, if you must, you must," Henry Fox would murmur philosophically. On a later occasion, when he heard that little Charles was extremely cross and disappointed because a garden wall that he had looked forward to seeing pulled down had been demolished in his absence, he promptly gave orders that the interesting stretch of brickwork should again be put up and once again destroyed. Similarly, when he was ready to go to school, the choice of an establishment was left to the boy's discretion. Charles had "determined," Henry informed a friend, to attend a fashionable boarding school at Wandsworth. Subsequently, he determined for Eton and for Hertford College, Oxford.

Although eighteenth-century parents were, on the whole, more kindly than those who overshadowed the mid-Victorian period, Henry Fox's behavior was considered a trifle ridiculous by the gentlest critics of his own age. The explanation, nevertheless, appears to have been a very simple one. Throughout his political career he was a remarkably unpopular man, long regarded, in a century accustomed to graft, as the most unscrupulous of contemporary jobbers. The office he had held was that of Paymaster General to His Majesty's forces at home and abroad. Nobody expected that an enterprising paymaster would fail to extract a profit from the public funds, lending and investing the surplus just as if he had been conducting an independent banking house, but Henry Fox's ingenious speculations were far too profitable to escape censure. During the course of the Seven Years'

By PETER QUENNELL

War, he had had the handling of nearly fifty million pounds, a sum (it has been pointed out) equivalent to a third of the national debt; and some millions were still in his hands when he retired to private life, where he spent his last days building and gardening and constructing bogus "Gothick" ruins.

No peaceful old age awaited him. He was pursued by a chorus of vituperation; and his fear that the world might break Charles's spirit evidently originated in his personal feelings—in his belief that he had been traduced and misjudged—combined perhaps with a secret sense of guilt. But Charles, though he lacked his father's acumen, had a better constitution and much more resilient nerves; for, whereas his paternal grandfather had been a self-made man, the product of a poor and undistinguished family, Charles was, through his mother, descended from a bastard son of King Charles II. Between this royal great-great-grandfather and the little boy born to Lady Caroline Fox and her ambitious husband on January 24, 1749, there was clearly a very close resemblance. Charles had inherited not only the Stuart looks—black hair and a peculiarly swart skin—but his ancestor's abounding love of pleasure, his robust worldly wisdom and easy affable charm. As an infant and a child, he had charmed his family; and his attractiveness did not decline with years. He delighted his friends at school, but he is said also to have demoralized them. Eighteenth-century Eton was never quite the same after he had made his mark there. When he was fourteen years old, his father decided that he should visit Paris, provided him with a daily supply of guineas to lose at the Parisian gaming rooms, and generally encouraged him to acquire a taste for all the fashionable modern vices. "He returned [we are told] so accomplished a gambler that the tone of the school suffered a long-enduring change for the worse. . . ." And it was as a passionate, almost a frenzied, gambler that he first amused and astonished London society.

By the time Henry Fox died in 1774—Charles was not yet twenty-six—he had already been obliged to settle card debts for his son that amounted to over a hundred thousand pounds, and many years were to pass before Charles gradually gave up play. High gaming, of course, is an end in itself, quite apart from the opportunity it affords of winning or of losing money. "I have a notion [Byron would write later] that Gamblers are as happy as most people, being always *excited*. Women, wine, fame, the table, even Ambition, *sate* now and then; but every turn of the card, and cast of the dice, keeps the Gamester alive. . . ." Charles needed excitement, even more perhaps than he needed easy money, and he happened to have been born in a period when gambling was the universal rage. The old and the middle-aged played with reckless abandon; but it was equally prevalent among the very young, who thought nothing (Horace Walpole records) of dropping "five, ten, fifteen thousand pounds in an evening . . . Lord Stavordale, not one and twenty, lost eleven thousand . . . last Tuesday, but recovered it by one great hand at hazard; he swore a great oath—'Now if I had been playing deep, I might have won millions.' "

Fox, however, was not only a gambler; he was a dandy, a sportsman, and a Member of Parliament. At this stage—it was never to happen again—he took considerable interest in the clothes he wore and adopted the costume of those men of fashion who were then admired or ridiculed as the *macaronis*, with red heels, "pigeon-wing" coiffure, a huge buttonhole bouquet ornamenting an exiguous cutaway coat, and a small hat, shaped like a shallow dish, perched upon the summit of the head. Such was the attire in which he was to be observed walking down St. James's Street, drinking and talking at White's, playing cards at Brooks's or Almack's. But London was not his whole existence: he was just as much in his element betting at a horse race—when his jockey appeared, he would climb into the saddle, jump the rails, and join the race himself—playing cricket under a summer sun, or pursuing a covey of partridge across the autumn fields. Yet, wherever he went, he continued to read voraciously (reading was one of his greatest joys), and he was remarkably assiduous, considering his other engagements, in his attendance at the House of Commons. Thanks to his father, he had gained a seat before he came of age; and he began to harangue the House, with growing effect, as early as 1769.

True, his interventions were sometimes unrehearsed; and Walpole describes a debate, on January 8, 1772, in which Fox's speech would have been more effective had he not "sat up playing hazard . . . from Tuesday evening 6th, till five in the afternoon of Wednesday 7th"—a game that increased his debts by the sum of £11,000. The sequel of the story is no less characteristic. After speaking, he had dined late and eventually adjourned to White's, "where he drank till seven the next morning; thence to Almack's, where he won £6000. . . ." Finally, between three and four, having presumably snatched a few hours' sleep, he entered the carriage at his door and went bowling off to Newmarket. Fox was never a man who tired easily; and, in his youth as in his later life, he seldom lost his high spirits. But meanwhile a tremendous load of debt was steadily accumulating. Duns threatened to remove his household chattels—once at least they completely stripped his house; and in a room set apart for the purpose, which he nicknamed his "Jerusalem Chamber," a crowd of moneylenders, who had helped to foot the bill, sat on duty patiently watching and waiting.

By his twenty-fifth year, Fox had earned the reputation of being one of the most dissipated men of his time; but simultaneously he was finding his feet as an accomplished orator and politician. Some of this he owed to his father's efforts. Far more decisive, however, was his natural strength of personality. His appearance—which would continue to inspire caricaturists for the next three decades—was itself commanding. Broadly built and not very tall, with a protuberant waistline and somewhat short legs, he had very bright eyes under heavy black eyebrows, a small, sensual, humorous mouth and a firm but deeply dimpled chin, which, like his large cheeks and huge circumference of jowl, invariably seemed to need shaving.

In a period of famous speakers, his method of delivery was pointed and vigorous rather than eloquent or graceful; but, although his speeches usually lacked polish, they were carried along by an irresistible flood of ideas, which helped to make him not only a splendid orator but, when he was at home among his friends, a tireless and enchanting talker. Edward Gibbon, who had often listened to him in the House of Commons, writes of Fox's "argumentative vehemence," which he contrasts with Lord North's consummate mastery of debate and Edmund Burke's "profuse and philosophic fancy"; and his beloved confidante, the Duchess of Devonshire (he claimed that she had the kindest heart in England), was dazzled both by his wit and learning and by his inimitable mixture of knowledge and fun. She had always thought, she informed her mother, "that the great merit of C. Fox is his amazing quickness in seizing any subject—he seems to have the particular talent of knowing more about what he is saying and with less pains than anybody else—his conversation is like a brilliant player of billiards, the strokes follow one another, piff paff."

In many respects, apart from his father's backing, Charles James Fox was an extraordinarily fortunate man. He had inherited immense vitality and an iron constitution, together with abundant natural gifts. During his lifetime, he encountered allies and adversaries whose intellect was the equal of his own, and the issues that confronted him as a politician were so large, urgent, and dramatic that they helped to bring out all his genius. The first, of course, was the major problem of American independence; the second, the question of India—sadly misgoverned, Fox and his party alleged, by the servants of the oppressive East India Company; the third, the French Revolution, which overshadowed the close of the eighteenth century just as the Russian Revolution was to overcloud the early twentieth. In his handling of each, he displayed sound good sense, coupled with a natural generosity of spirit as well as a measure of sentiment that he owed to his literary education. Herodotus was among his favorite authors. Once, when, after a night at the tables, he seemed to have lost his last shilling, he was discovered alone in his rooms placidly browsing through a volume of the *History*; and Herodotus's account of how the free Greek cities had defied and broken the vast armies of tyrannical Asia helped to shape the imaginative point of view from which he regarded the problems of the current age. As a Man of Feeling, he hated oppression and detested the idea of military coercion; as a man of the world, he doubted the practical efficacy of any settlement imposed by brute force.

Thus, in Fox the American colonists found a courageous and determined champion. At the very beginning of the struggle, it is true, he appeared to have taken sides with Lord North and even delivered speeches approving the clo-sure of the port of Boston; but his attitude soon became more liberal as the issues involved became increasingly definite. It is difficult to credit the story, afterwards propagated by his political foes, that "if an idle quarrel had not happened between him and Lord North, we might have seen him a supporter of the American War" and "a champion for the prerogative of the Crown. . . ." His original motives may well have been mixed—other statesmen in history have reached the right conclusions for the wrong reasons—but once he had embraced the American cause, it engaged all his powers of feeling and thought. At this stage, he gained a magnificent ally, a man of equally outstanding gifts. Edmund Burke and Charles James Fox might have been specially designed to run in double harness, with complementary but contrasted talents and the same passionate devotion to their country's interests.

The contrast they presented was striking. Some years before war broke out between the Colonies and Great Britain, Horace Walpole, attracted by what he had lately heard of young Charles Fox's growing fame, went down to the House of Commons to attend an important debate on a bill that Fox was introducing. Burke, Walpole tells us, "made a long and fine oration," two-thirds of which "resembled the beginning of a book on speculative doctrines, and yet argument was not the forte of it. Charles Fox, who had been running about the House talking to different persons and scarce listening to Burke, rose with amazing spirit and memory, answered both Lord North and Burke. . . . His words flowed rapidly but he had nothing of Burke's variety of language or correctness. . . . Yet his arguments were far more shrewd. . . . Burke was indefatigable, learned, and versed in every branch of eloquence. Fox was dissolute, dissipated. . . . He was that very morning returned from Newmarket, where he had lost some thousands of pounds the preceding day. He had stopped at Hockerel, where he found company, had sat up drinking all night, and had not been to bed when he came to move his bill, which he had not even drawn up. This was genius—almost inspiration."

Both men were destined to show their genius in the long series of debates on American affairs. In Lord North—that "unfortunate Minister," as he used to call himself—they had a worthy opponent, capable of standing up to their combined assault, for North, although a wrong-headed statesman, was a master of parliamentary tactics. Although his tears were inclined to flow freely during his painful audiences with the King, and in the House of Commons he often slept, "heaving backwards and forwards like a great turtle," no historian would today describe him as either a coward or a sluggard, an ignoramus or a knave. Fox had begun by sounding the note of sober common sense: the system of taxation proposed was unjust, absurd, unnecessary; the government had denied that it was concerned with imposing a commercial regulation or safeguarding a source of revenue. If its object was simply to assert its rights, he said, "it is only done with a view to irritate and declare war against the Americans, which, if you persist in, I am clearly of opinion you will effect, or force them into open rebellion."

To the protests of Fox and Burke, Lord Chatham, in the House of Lords, added the solemn warning of a decrepit Elder Statesman: "We shall be forced ultimately to retreat; let us retreat while we can, not when we must. I say we must necessarily undo these violent oppressive acts; they must be repealed—you will repeal them; I stake my reputation on it. . . ." But Lord North and his government were now committed to a coercive policy. The first shots of the war were heard at Lexington, and for the next eight years, until 1783, Fox and his allies continued to deliver a succession of furious attacks against the obstinate, supine figure tossing uneasily upon the front bench. They tried reason; they appealed to the love of justice; they exhausted all the resources of personal satire and invective. North, Fox exclaimed, was "a lump of deformity and disease, of folly and wickedness, of ignorance and temerity. . . ." At the same time, they paid anxious attention to the progress of the American colonists' struggle; and in 1776, when American fortunes seemed to have reached a very low ebb, Fox wrote to a friend, Lord Ossory: "Whatever happens, for God's sake let us all resolve to stick by them as handsomely (or more so) in their adversity as we have done in their glory, and still maintain the Whig cause, however discredited by defeat, to be the only true principle for this country."

Meanwhile, although his public passions were hotly aroused, Fox did not change his private habits. He still gambled from dusk to dawn (Walpole observed that "he was seldom in bed before five in the morning, nor out of it before two at noon"); he still borrowed of all who would lend, including the waiters at Brooks's and friendly chairmen in St. James's Street; and a horde of observant duns still thronged the celebrated "Jerusalem Chamber." His appearance, nevertheless, had undergone a transformation. No longer was he a red-heeled dandy, sporting an odd little French hat; his natural eccentricity had degenerated into downright slovenliness—his shock of black hair was usually uncombed, and he wore a plain blue coat and a simple buff waistcoat, in imitation, it was said, of the colors of the American colonists. Particularly unconventional was the effect he produced when he had just emerged from bed at noon; and we have a description of Fox greeting his friends—among whom was the elegant Prince of Wales—at breakfast: "His bristly, black person, and shagged breast quite open and rarely purified by any ablutions, was wrapped in a foul linen night gown, and his bushy hair dishevelled."

But Fox, despite his forbidding looks, was always capable of pleasing women. He had declined to marry any of the heiresses whom his well-wishers at various times put forward (he hoped Charles would marry, sighed his father: for then, on at least one night of his life, he would probably get to bed at a reasonable hour). But he had been the lover of the beautiful Perdita Robinson, recently the Prince's love; and in 1783 he made a lasting conquest of the no less beautiful Mrs. Armistead, a rich and famous demimondaine who adored him faithfully as long as he lived and whom, to the perturbation of his friends, he finally married in 1795. Elizabeth Armistead was cultivated and intelligent, as well as seductive and warm-hearted; and she owned a delightful country cottage, St. Ann's Hill in Surrey, not very far from London, where he passed many hours of happy leisure. Their association had a pleasantly domestic side and shocked no one except Edward Gibbon. In October, 1788, they visited the historian at his Swiss retreat, and Gibbon commented that Elizabeth Armistead's unquestionable wit and grace were "not sufficient to excuse the scandalous impropriety of showing her to all Europe." But then, Gibbon was one of Nature's celibates; while Fox, in everything apart from the name,

Carlo Khan's triumphal Entry into Leadenhall Street

In James Sayer's famous cartoon, Fox rides up to the door of India House astride an elephant (with the unhappy face of Lord North) led by Burke. On Fox's banner, "The Man of the People" has been changed to "King of Kings" in Greek.

was now an affectionate and attentive husband.

Little by little, he gave up the habit of gambling, but he never abandoned his career of public service. Few men have had a greater gift for relaxing pleasurably in a library or garden; yet, when a summons arrived from Westminster, he was always prepared to hasten back. "I love idleness so much and so dearly [he announced], that I have hardly the heart to say a word against it; but something is due to one's station in life, something to friendship, something to the country." In a study of this length it is impossible to trace all the vicissitudes of Fox's political career or to explain, for example, why or how, at the end of the American conflict, he formed a brief alliance with Lord North, whom he had previously stigmatized as a "lump of deformity." He was an active member of the House of Commons for more than thirty-seven years; but as a modern historian pointed out not so long ago, "his ministerial career is counted in months . . . rather than in years . . . he held high Cabinet office for three months in 1782, eight months in 1783, and seven months in 1806—a year and a half in all." As a minister he was remarkably diligent, and astonished his critics by his close attention to business, but it was as the spearhead of the Opposition that he scored his most conspicuous triumphs —as the scourge of the government and the foe of the Court, presently as the bellicose Man of the People.

In the former roles, he had staunchly opposed the government's handling of the American colonists and had deplored the sovereign's political influence, thus drawing down on his head the fierce enmity of King George III. His next campaign was directed at British commercial imperialism overseas. Again the criticism he delivered was founded on both sense and sentiment, and again his chief ally in the fight was the philosophic theorist Edmund Burke. But neither Fox nor Burke seem to have paused to reflect that a public-spirited crusade might have been launched as a selfish private vendetta, and that Philip Francis's feud with Warren Hastings made his highly colored denunciations possibly a trifle suspect. Still, there was no doubt that the servants of the East India Company *had* exploited and misgoverned their Indian vassals, and that the Company's administration needed to be controlled and regularized. Fox's attack on the Company earned him the nickname of "Carlo Khan"; and a popular contemporary cartoon represented him riding an elephant, led by Burke, also wearing Eastern clothes and blowing a trumpet, toward the Company's offices in Leadenhall Street.

The impeachment of Warren Hastings, the first governor general of British India, began on February 13, 1788, amid scenes that resembled the opening night of some stupendous theatrical production. The boxes and galleries were densely crowded; before the third sitting, tickets were sold for the sum of fifty guineas apiece. Burke opened the proceedings with one of the finest speeches that he ever delivered; he spoke continuously for four days and wound up so eloquently that the lovely Mrs. Sheridan collapsed in a swoon. He was followed by Fox (ladies who had come to hear him struggled out of bed at six o'clock and, once they had gained admittance to Westminster Hall, waited miserably shivering from nine till eleven) and by Sheridan, whose superb feats of oratory again caused Mrs. Sheridan to swoon. The result of the impeachment was inconclusive: Hastings was at length acquitted in 1795. But thanks to the efforts of Fox and his friends, the treatment of subject races—Indian and African alike—had become a vital parliamentary issue.

Somewhat more ill-advised had been Fox's intervention in the troublesome affairs of the Prince of Wales. The future George IV admired and flattered Fox, largely because the King, whom the Prince had always loathed, so cordially abominated him; and it fell to the Whig leader not only to approach Parliament about the young man's mountainous and pressing debts—they totaled at that moment nearly £200,000—but to deny that he had contracted a clandestine

CONTINUED ON PAGE 124

A RIGHT HONORABLE alias a Sans Culotte

In one of the many caricatures depicting Fox as a dangerous advocate of revolutionary principles, Cruikshank gave him a split personality—one half a portly but proper English gentleman, the other a ravening sans-culotte brandishing a club.

101

"SUDDEN SHOWER AT OHASHI" BY ICHIRYUSAI HIROSHIGE

"YELLOW AND PURPLE" BY TAKUMI SHINAGAWA

By JAMES A. MICHENER

AN EASTERN ART GOES WESTERN

The traditional Japanese wood block is being revolutionized by influences from across the seas. A prominent collector describes the process and introduces a portfolio of new prints

In these days the intelligent Westerner can scarcely avoid the impact that Oriental art is exerting upon our culture. One hard-working actress, surveying the plethora of Broadway plays and musicals with Japanese and Chinese subjects, recently complained, "This year a girl can't find a job unless she's flat-chested and slant-eyed." Oriental influence is felt in music, dance, architecture, and graphic arts. Yet at the same time, the art of the West, for its part, is exerting a strong reciprocal influence upon the Orient, and this is nowhere embodied more vividly than in the traditional art of Japanese print making, where the results have been revolutionary.

It was, of course, through its own traditional prints that the art of Japan first influenced Europe. A collection of them reached the continent in the middle of the last century—to be called by some "those magnificent scraps of paper"—and rarely has the art of one nation arrived in another with more exquisite timing. For these prints seized the imaginations of many major French artists then in search of fresh inspiration.

Camille Pissarro, Edgar Degas, Claude Monet, Edouard Manet, and particularly the American Mary Cassatt have left us verbal and artistic records testifying to the impact of the Japanese works. Today it would be possible to assemble a respectable exhibition of impressionist paintings which contain copies of Japanese prints or make significant use of Japanese symbols. One of the outstanding items would be Vincent van Gogh's literal copy in oil of the famous print by Ichiryusai Hiroshige shown on the opposite page.

103

It must be admitted that this impact of Japanese prints on the West could not have occurred had not European artists already launched experiments that paved the way for it. The nourishment of classicism and romanticism was growing weak. Photography had taught new lessons in design; lithography had revitalized the print; and men like Eugène Delacroix, J. M. W. Turner, and John Constable had seen the value of brilliant, pure color applied to the canvas. Ideas were already in ferment, and some great conclusion was inevitable. But it is reasonable to argue that the Japanese helped. Many Western artists have testified to the joy with which they discovered the Japanese print, with its emphasis on decorative quality, its fresh use of line and color, its audacious foreshortening, and particularly the daring manner in which its principal subject was so often placed off-center. On another level, the graphic artists of Europe were delighted by the effective way in which the Japanese print utilized titles and text as part of the over-all design of a work of art. As a result the posters of Europe were revolutionized.

Yet this artistic movement was by no means exclusively an East-to-West affair. For although the influence of the Japanese print was great upon the impressionists, and also upon men like Whistler, Bonnard, Toulouse-Lautrec, and Matisse, the impact of *their* work upon Japan was to become perhaps even greater. It is obvious that Van Gogh learned from the Japanese, for we have his copy work to prove it, but it will also be clear from the prints which accompany this essay that Van Gogh, his colleagues and successors have had a profound influence upon the Japanese.

To understand precisely how this interchange came about, let us go back to Edo, the ancient name for Tokyo, in 1857. It was in that year that Hiroshige's wood-block print *Sudden Shower at Ohashi* was offered to the Edo public. As soon as it was issued, it was recognized as an important work.

Popular choice made it the masterwork of what was to be Hiroshige's last great series of landscape prints. This set of one hundred and eighteen was entitled *One Hundred Famous Views of Edo;* the discrepancy in numbers was not important, for when a Japanese artist found that the public was beginning to like one of his series, he sensibly crammed more prints into it, regardless of its formal title. Thus Hokusai's well-received series, *Thirty-six Views of Fuji,* finally embraced forty-six rather pleasing subjects.

One of the things that accounted for the success of *Sudden Shower at Ohashi* was its perfect exemplification of rain in nature. Observe how the lines slant down from two different directions, suggesting the conflict of a storm. It also exemplifies some of the lessons that were to be learned by Europeans: the use of flat color applied over broad areas, the impressionistic rendering of reality, and above all the representation of nature by means of planes.

We must now jump about fifty years to the beginning of the twentieth century. In Paris the results of the East-to-West exchange have become stabilized in the masterpieces of the French school. But in Tokyo its reciprocal effects have not yet begun to be felt, and meanwhile the historic Japanese wood-block print has fallen into disrepute. Listen to the type of complaint that was being made by amateur Japanese critics in the early 1900's:

"How can you honestly call this man Hiroshige an artist? What did he do, actually? I'll tell you what he did and what they're still trying to make us do. Take this famous print of his, *Sudden Shower at Ohashi.* Hiroshige sketched this in black ink on a very thin piece of absorbent paper. And when I say sketch, I mean just that. He never applied any color. In many respects he didn't even finish his drawing. Those rain lines we admire: he never bothered to rule them in—just indicated them. The work of art we see in that bridge today, he really had very little to do with.

"Because as soon as his sketch was completed, he handed it to a professional wood carver, and that was the end of it, so far as Hiroshige was concerned. This mechanic with his knives carved one master block plus a set of eight or nine companion blocks, one for each of the major colors. I doubt that Hiroshige himself ever saw these blocks. He certainly would never have been able to carve one of them himself. He didn't begin to have enough carving skill for that.

"Well, in due time the set of nine or ten blocks was delivered to a professional printer, not to Hiroshige. This mechanical artisan mixed the proper colors, applied them to the blocks, and struck off the finished work. Here again I doubt that Hiroshige even saw what the printer was doing. The first time he saw a finished print, the kind that the Europeans became so excited about, was when his publisher showed him one in the salesroom. And when Hiroshige did see a finished job he had to confess that he was not responsible for the actual carved lines, or for the paper, or for the exact colors, or for the printing. All he had provided was the sketch. Now really, under the circumstances, ought you to call Hiroshige an artist?"

Arguments like this agitated the artistic world of Japan for many years. Although there were some who maintained, "This is the tradition of Japan and it must be preserved," their defense of the old techniques was routed when one looked at the actual content of what was being done in the name of ancient art. Japanese prints consisted mainly of sickly-sweet landscapes, coy girls in kimonos, and the inevitable view of Mount Fuji in the snow. If the techniques were moribund, the content was equally so.

At this low point in the fortunes of the Japanese print, a vital new concept exploded across Japan, and curiously enough it came from those very European artists whose own moribund artistic concepts in the 1850's had been so vividly affected by the Japanese. In 1913 and 1914, landmark exhibitions were held in Tokyo of works by Vincent

TEXT CONTINUED ON PAGE 113

"OBJET Nº 2" BY KOSHIRO ONCHI

"THE ROAD" BY TADASHIGE ONO

"TWO HANIWA" BY KIYOSHI SAITO

"STAND ON THE SNOW GORGE" BY UMETARO AZECH

"DEEP ATTACHMENT" BY GEN YAMAGUCHI

"WOODS" BY HODAKA YOSHIDA

"SAND GARDEN" BY OKIIE HASHIMOT

"CHILD GOD" BY HODAKA YOSHIDA

"SLEEPING CRANE" BY TADASHI NAKAYAMA

"BUDDHA HEAD" BY UN'ICHI HIRATSUKA

TEXT CONTINUED FROM PAGE 104

van Gogh. Promptly thereafter paintings and prints by men like Monet, Pissarro, and Bonnard were seen there, and in the face of such powerful new art, the old, pretty world of the Japanese print collapsed. The young men who had been protesting against the mechanical techniques of the Hiroshige school cried, "To be free an artist must not only draw the original sketch. He is obligated to carve his blocks with his own hands. He must select his own paper, mix his paints to his own taste, and do the printing himself." In addition, these young men were determined that their work show the sweeping freedom of subject matter, form, and color that marked the work of the Europeans. Thus a body of ideas that the Japanese had originally sent to Paris to help save European art now returned a hundredfold to help save a Japanese art.

Look at the print on the first page of this portfolio. It was executed in 1954 by Koshiro Onchi, who entitled it in French, *Objet Nᵒ 2*. After sketching his idea for this print, Onchi himself carved the blocks, mixed his paints in little cups borrowed from his wife's kitchen, searched Tokyo till he found paper exactly to his taste, and then did the printing with his own hands. Furthermore, instead of using the time-honored cherry plank upon which the classical masterpieces of Japanese wood-block art had been built, Onchi picked up some scraps of timber left over from the building of his daughter's house, and, to obtain the striking over-all design in red, used hunks of household charcoal sawed in half to reveal the secret designs. In this subtle wedding of wood in its two forms, Onchi achieved a masterpiece. It is, I believe, one of the foremost bits of graphic art produced in the world in the last fifty years. In time, Koshiro Onchi, a brave and a great man who died in 1955, will be recognized as the peer of men like Georges Braque, Georges Rouault, and Paul Klee.

Fortunately, we do not have to speculate about the influence of European masters upon men like Onchi, for he stated, "My teachers were Wassily Kandinsky, Oskar Kokoschka, and those Van Gogh exhibitions in 1913 and 1914."

Like the rest of the modern school, Onchi paid special homage to the inspired Norwegian Edvard Munch, whose stark black-and-white woodcuts appealed to Japanese tastes. Munch's influence can be seen in the print shown here by Tadashige Ono (page 106). *The Road* is clearly a restatement of the Norwegian's impressive woodcut *Anxiety*. And here again we need not depend upon detective work to reach this conclusion, for Ono has recently published an essay reporting the debt of Japanese artists to Munch. It is the kind of obligation that men like Onchi and Ono have always been proud to acknowledge, for sharing the ideas of leading Europeans has made the Japanese feel a part of the international world of art.

One can see the influence of Pablo Picasso and Diego Rivera upon Hodaka Yoshida, whose Mexican motifs, as exemplified in *Child God* (page 111), were the result of a trip to that country. And the international style—whose subject matter has not derived from any specific locale—is well illustrated by Gen Yamaguchi's *Deep Attachment*. Such prints could have been designed in any country in the world. They exhibit nothing that is inescapably Japanese.

In fact, of the nine contemporary prints shown in this portfolio, none has a style which marks it as exclusively Japanese, and only two contain any pictorial elements that I would be able to identify as typical of Japan. Kiyoshi Saito's *Two Haniwa* depicts clay burial figures which are peculiar to the Orient, while Okiie Hashimoto's *Sand Garden* reports upon a landscaping tradition which is not only peculiar to Japan but is also one of its chief artistic accomplishments—the rocks representing the islands of Japan

113

and the rippling sand the motion of the restless sea. As far as the subject matter is concerned, all the other prints could just as well have been produced in Austria or Canada. Better than words, they symbolize Japan's adoption of the full international style, with its elements of expressionism and abstractionism.

There are some who lament this abandonment of the old, and their protests merit attention. But I do object when they proceed to argue that Japanese artists should not utilize an international subject matter or style but should continue turning out prints in the strict Hokusai-Hiroshige tradition of colorful landscapes. It is true that foreign travelers have grown accustomed to such prints, but to restrict contemporary artists to such subject matter would condemn Japanese prints to the sterility of the early 1900's, when the classic tradition was found to be bankrupt.

On the other hand, if Japan had carelessly allowed one of its most authentic artistic traditions to lapse through indifference, a cultural loss would have been suffered. From 1650 to 1850, Japanese artists produced what is now recognized as the finest color wood-block printing ever achieved, and fortunately today's Japanese artists do respect the vital parts of that tradition, even though they have forcefully broken away from its inhibiting limitations.

In the prints of this portfolio, see how handsomely the effect of wood has been utilized in the Onchi, the Saito, and the two Yoshida works. This feeling for wood has been inherited from the earlier tradition of Japanese print making; so also is the use of flat color in broad design, as exemplified in the works by Azechi and Yamaguchi, while the exhilarating rhythms of Nakayama's poetic crane carry on the delicate line produced by the classical masters.

Contemporary Japanese wood-block artists thus combine the best of the international style with the permanent components of a traditional Japanese method. In doing so, they have won approval around the world.

It is therefore somewhat ironic that in Japan itself judgment about them is cautiously reserved. For example, Koshiro Onchi, who seems well on his way to an international reputation of the first category, remains largely unknown in Japan outside a small coterie in Tokyo. A forceful and dynamic artist like Shinagawa, whose study in yellow and purple is shown on page 103, is largely ignored at home. A print by Yamaguchi, which wins first prize in Lugano against competition from all countries, will sell well in America and Europe, but not conspicuously at home.

This indifference is nothing new. It is merely a continuation of understandable prejudices that have always existed in Japan against wood-block prints. The canon of Japanese art dictates simplicity, austerity, and a kind of patrician aloofness. Paintings and drawings that conform to this canon are much prized in Japan and are kept in private homes rather than in public museums. Not many have been allowed to escape to the West, and one can visit numerous museums without coming into contact with that ultimate art which the Japanese cherish. Thanks to Ernest Fenollosa, an amazing young man from Harvard who went to Japan in the 1870's as a college professor and who stayed to become the world's leading expert on Japanese art, the museum at Boston has a choice collection of real masterpieces; and by dint of hard collecting in this century, Chicago, Honolulu, and Kansas City have also acquired respectable examples. But for the most part, Westerners have had to approach Japanese art through the wood-block print.

This is ironic, for the Japanese connoisseur, whose ideal is a subdued ink-brush drawing of a single bird perched on the vaguely indicated branch of a shadowy pine, has always looked askance at the garish prints of Hokusai and Hiroshige. He has never quite recovered from the shock of what happened when the plebeian wood blocks of Japan exploded in Paris, and he continues to be amazed that a man like Hiroshige could have influenced a great painter like Van Gogh. Few sophisticated Japanese collectors have ever bothered with prints, and the prejudice continues. It stems from three facts: (1) prints originally stressed prostitutes, actors, and other "unacceptable" social content; (2) the landscapes of Hokusai and Hiroshige were considered merely as picture post cards of travel scenes and were not taken seriously; (3) prints suffered from the drawback of having been issued cheaply and in prolific editions.

Of course, when masterful collections had been assembled in Paris, London, Berlin, and particularly in Boston and Chicago, and when critics throughout the world acknowledged the excellence of Japanese prints, collections were belatedly assembled in Japan.

But the important thing about Japanese prints is not their popular acceptance at home or lack of it. In Japan today perhaps half a hundred capable wood-block artists are practicing one of Japan's most distinctive arts. These men make modest livings and, while doing so, add luster to the international world of art. The reader, by looking closely at the prints themselves, will spot one of the distinguishing characteristics of this dedicated group. Most prints are signed in Western rather than Japanese lettering, and many are titled that way, too. The pattern was established by men like Onchi, who went as far as to spell his name in German because he felt that the music of Brahms and Beethoven had shown him the way to freedom. Once, when I asked Onchi about the appropriateness of his doing this, he explained, "We are no longer content to be provincial Japanese artists. We are determined to be full-fledged citizens of the world of art, and our signatures in the European manner proclaim this fact." Judging from the acceptance which the world is according them, they have attained their goal.

Best known for his tales and novels, James A. Michener is also a student and collector of Japanese prints, and has written of them in The Floating World *and other studies.*

The pencil is mightier than the lance, for Sir James used it to turn a gang of sixth-century hoods into clean-living Boy Scouts

HOW TO MAKE THE ROUND TABLE SQUARE

Not long ago, while turning through the furthest and most neglected shelf in my library, I rediscovered a dusty volume I had long forgotten. It was my copy of the 1923 edition of *King Arthur and His Knights* by Sir James Knowles, K.C.V.O., first published in 1862 and dedicated to Lord Tennyson. I recalled it as one of the most exciting books of my childhood, and since my wife informs me that I have never left that privileged state, I now turned the pages again in pleasurable anticipation. Soon I became so involved in Sir James's florescent prose that my head began to swim.

"Would you like a drink?" my wife asked.

"Verily," I said. "Forsooth and yea." She brought me Scotch and soda.

"Grammercy," I said.

I read on through the tales that had enchanted my boyhood and then turned to the preface where the author, in giving his sources, explains: "It [the book] is little else than an abridgement of Sir Thomas Malory's version of them as printed by Caxton." If I had read this statement at all at the time, I suppose I had taken it on faith—anyway I had not gone back to William Caxton's printing of Malory's *Morte d'Arthur* (first edition, 1485) to check with the original. My curiosity aroused, this I did now, finding a copy of Malory left over from a Freshman course in English. I also found that what Sir James had done to Sir Thomas shouldn't happen to a brachet (Malory for dog).

Sir James emasculated not only Malory's prose but his heroes as well. Let us take for example the incidents leading up to King Arthur's birth. Here is Sir James's version:

Now, when Uther Pendragon had passed through all the land, and settled it—and even voyaged into all the countries of the Scots, and tamed the fierceness of that rebel people—he came to London, and ministered justice there. And it befell at a certain great banquet and high feast which the king made at Easter-tide, there came, with many earls and other barons, Gorloïs, Duke of Cornwall, and his wife Igerna, who was the most famous beauty in all Britain. And soon thereafter, Gorloïs being slain in battle, Uther determined to make Igerna his own wife. But in order to do this, and enable him to come to her—for she was shut up in the high castle of Tintagil, on the furthest coast of Cornwall—the king sent for Merlin, to take counsel with him and to pray his help. This, therefore, Merlin promised him on one condition—namely, that the king should give him up the first son born of the marriage. For Merlin by his arts foreknew that this firstborn should be the long-wished prince, King Arthur.

Now this isn't the way it was at all, and Sir James very well knows it. If you want to know what really happened, turn back to Sir Thomas:

It befell in the days of Uther Pendragon, when he was king of all England, and so reigned, that there was a mighty duke in Cornwall that held war against him long time. And the duke was called the duke of Tintagil. And so by means King Uther sent for this duke, charging him to bring his wife with him, for she was called a fair lady, and a passing wise, and her name was called Igraine. So when the duke and his wife were come unto the king, by the means of great lords they were accorded both: the king liked and loved this lady well, and he made them great cheer out of measure, and desired to have lain by her. But she was a passing good woman, and would not assent unto the king. And then she

By KENNETH R. MORGAN

115

Tristram at work: a 13th-century tile

told the duke her husband, and said, I suppose that we were sent for that I should be dishonoured, wherefore, husband, I counsel you, that we depart from hence suddenly, that we may ride all night unto our own castle.

When the king discovers that his guests have sneaked out on him he is "wonderly wroth" and rushes down to Cornwall to drag them back. The duke has shut himself up in the castle of Terrabil and his wife in the castle of Tintagil, ten miles away. After a few days it appears that Uther's siege—or, if you will, suit—isn't going too well. He sends for Merlin, who exercises his creepy powers with a convenient lack of scruple:

Now make you ready, said Merlin, this night ye shall lie with Igraine in the castle of Tintagil, and ye shall be like the duke her husband. . . . But wayte ye make not many questions with her nor her men . . . and so hie you to bed, and rise not on the morn till I come to you . . . so this was done as they devised. But the duke of Tintagil espied how the king rode from the siege of Terrabil, and therefore that night he issued out of the castle at a postern . . . [and] was slain or-ever the king came at the castle of Tintagil. So after the death of the duke, King Uther lay with Igraine more than three hours after his death, and begat on her that night Arthur. . . .

In other words (*not* Sir James's), King Uther covets his neighbor's wife, gets his local wizard to see that the man is killed, and goes to bed with the lady in the guise of her dead husband. Igraine, as it turns out—for all that she was "a passing good woman"—is not troubled with delicate sensibilities: she and Uther are married thirteen days after the funeral and then settle down to have a good laugh over the whole thing.

According to Sir James, Lancelot du Lac "had the greatest name of any knight in all the world, and by high and low was he the most honoured of all men." Very well. But what does

Sir Thomas say? We turn the *un*abridged pages of the *Morte d'Arthur,* and here is the noble knight—riding out of the woods at dusk and espying a small tent pitched in a glade:

By my faith, said Sir Launcelot, in that pavilion will I lodge all this night, and so there he alit down, and tied his horse to the pavilion, and there he unarmed him, and there he found a bed, and laid him therein and fell on sleep sadly.

Then within an hour there came a knight to whom the pavilion ought, and he weened that his leman [mistress] had lain in that bed, and so he laid him down beside Sir Launcelot, and took him in his arms and began to kiss him. And when Sir Launcelot felt a rough beard kissing him, he started out of the bed lightly, and the other knight after him, and either of them gat their swords in their hands, and out at the pavilion door went the knight of the pavilion, and Sir Launcelot followed him, and there by a little slake Sir Launcelot wounded him sore, nigh unto the death. And then he yielded him to Sir Launcelot, and so he granted him, so that he would tell him why he came in to the bed. Sir, said the knight, the pavilion is mine own, and there this night I had assigned my lady to have slept with me, and now I am likely to die of this wound.

That me repenteth, said Launcelot. . . .

Lancelot repenteth, but is that enough? Here is this poor devil, coming home after a hard day of breaking lances and cleaving skulls, looking forward to the happy assignation— and what awaits him? Not his mistress but an unknown lout in his bed who jumps up and wounds him "nigh unto death." A pretty end to the evening.

When it comes to Lancelot's love for King Arthur's wife, Guinevere, Sir James would have us believe that it was all very spiritual. We must turn back to Malory for the truth:

Then Sir Launcelot took his sword in his hand, and privily went to a place where he had espied a ladder toforehand, and that he took under his arm, and bare it through the garden, and set it up to the window, and there anon the queen was ready to meet him. And then they made either to other their complaints of many diverse things, and then Sir Launcelot wished that he might have come in to her. Wit ye well, said the queen, I would as fain as ye, that ye might come in to me. Would ye, madam, said Sir Launcelot, with your heart that I were with you? Yea, truly, said the queen. . . . and then he set his hands upon the bars of iron, and he pulled at them with such a might that he brast them clene out of the stone walls, and therewithal one of the bars of iron cut the brawn of his hands throughout to the bone; and then he leapt into the chamber to the queen. . . . So, to pass upon this tale, Sir Launcelot went unto bed with the queen, and he took no force of his hurt hand, but took his pleasance and his liking until it was in the dawning of the day; and wit ye well he slept not but watched, and when he saw his time that he might tarry no longer he took his leave and departed at the window, and put it together as well as he might again, and so departed unto his own chamber; and there he told Sir Lavaine how he was hurt. . . . and so the queen lay long in her bed until it was nine of the clock. Then Sir Meliagrance went to the queen's chamber, and found her ladies there ready clothed. Jesu mercy, said Sir Meliagrance, what aileth you, madam, that ye sleep thus long? And right therewithal he opened the curtain for to behold her; and then was he ware where she lay, and all the sheet and the pillow was bebled with the blood of Sir Launcelot and of his hurt hand.

Leaving aside some nagging questions about the queen's

accessibility, it is clear that Sir Lancelot was a pretty clumsy lover—and a cad besides. Why does he have to go and peach to Sir Lavaine? However, a bit further on in the story he gets a little of what's coming to him—not that you'd ever learn it from Sir James Knowles, K.C.V.O. According to Malory, Lancelot has fallen asleep beside a well when along comes a damsel hunting deer with bow and arrow. The deer gets between Lancelot and the huntress—but it is better to let Sir Thomas tell the story:

. . . And there she [the huntress] came stiffly and found the hind, and she put a broad arrow in her bow, and shot at the hind, and over shot the hind; and so by misfortune the arrow smote Sir Launcelot in the thick of the buttock, over the barbs. When Sir Launcelot felt himself so hurt, he hurled up woodly, and saw the lady that had smitten him. . . . Alas, said Sir Launcelot, ye have mischieved me. And so the lady departed, and Sir Launcelot as he might pulled out the arrow, and left that head still in his buttock, and so he went weakly to the hermitage. . . . Then with great pain the hermit gat the arrow out of Sir Launcelot's buttock, and the wound was passing sore, and unhappily smitten, for it was in such a place that he might not sit in no saddle.

Unhorsed, he no longer claims our attention. But there was another brave knight, if we are to believe Sir James Knowles, who was even more virtuous than Lancelot. His name was Tristram of Lyonesse. As a boy I envisioned him as a combination of Red Grange, Babe Ruth, General Custer, and my local scoutmaster. Most of his troubles stemmed from a quarrel with his uncle, King Mark, but Sir James seems curiously vague about the cause of it:

[Tristram] came again to King Mark's court, and there lived in great joy and pleasure, till within a while the king grew jealous of his fame, and of the love and favour shown him by all damsels. And as long as King Mark lived, he never after loved Sir Tristram, though there was much fair speech between them.

Malory is more instructive. He says nothing about the "fair speech" between them, but quite a bit about Sir Segwarides's wife:

Then by the license of King Meliodas, his father, he [Tristram] returned again unto the court of King Mark, and there he lived in great joy long time, until at last there befell a jealousy and an unkindness betwixt King Mark and Sir Tristram, for they loved both one lady. And she was an earl's wife that hight Sir Segwarides.

The fact that she already has a husband is no deterrent to uncle and nephew in their assault on her virtue. Nor is it, indeed, to the lady. She invites Sir Tristram to her chamber, jealous King Mark creases him with a spear, and—not stopping to stanch his wound—Sir Tristram repairs to his rendezvous where he bleeds all over his eager victim's sheets (an inescapable *motif*, apparently, in Arthurian romance). Sir Segwarides, finding his wife's bed "troubled and broken," becomes a nuisance, and there is nothing for it but to have Sir Tristram smite him through the waist.

Shortly after this untidy affair, King Mark becomes enamored of Isoud, daughter of the king of Ireland. A slow learner, he sends his nephew to Ireland to escort her back to Cornwall. En route the two young people decide to have a drink, and help themselves to the contents of a flask containing a love potion intended for King Mark and his bride. The result has been described at unnecessary length by Richard Wagner. But let us take Malory's version:

Then Sir Tristram used daily and nightly to go to Queen Isoud when he might, and ever Sir Andred his cousin watched him night and day for to take him with La Beale Isoud. And so upon a night Sir Andred espied the hour and the time when Sir Tristram went to his lady. Then Sir Andred gat unto him twelve knights, and at midnight he set upon Sir Tristram secretly and suddenly, and there Sir Tristram was taken naked abed with La Beale Isoud, and then was he bound hand and foot. . . .

Tristram escapes, Wagner notwithstanding, and Isoud goes back to King Mark. Our hero lands in Brittany and marries another girl with the same first name, Isoud La Blanche Mains. Unfortunately, on his wedding night, just as he is about to burn on the bed of passion, Tristram has a sudden lowering of temperature:

And so when they were abed both, Sir Tristram remembered him of his old lady La Beale Isoud. And then he took such a thought suddenly that he was all dismayed, and other cheer made he none but with clipping and kissing; as for other fleshly lusts Sir Tristram never thought nor had ado with her: such mention maketh the French book; also it maketh mention that the lady weened there had been no pleasure but kissing and clipping.

It seems rather too bad that Tristram couldn't have remembered his "old lady" before the marriage instead of giving poor Blanche Mains only the meager reward of kissing and "clipping" (explained not by Sir James or Sir Thomas but by Webster as "embracing, hugging"). Lancelot, for one, wouldn't have believed in that "other-cheer-made-he-none"

Sir Tristram teaches La Beale Isoud to harp

Tristram and companions go to feast

bit, though he unaccountably finds this marriage of Tristram's distinctly non-U:

Then said Sir Launcelot: Fie upon him, untrue knight to his lady that so noble a knight as Sir Tristram is should be found to his first lady false, La Beale Isoud, Queen of Cornwall.

Eventually Tristram manages to convince Lancelot that his marriage didn't count and that he still loves his aunt. This makes everything all right. When Tristram finally spirits the first Isoud out of Cornwall and into England, Lancelot turns his castle over to the happy couple so that they can set up housekeeping.

And so Sir Launcelot brought Sir Tristram and La Beale Isoud unto Joyous Gard, that was his own castle, that he had won with his own hands. And there Sir Launcelot put them in to welde for their own. And wit ye well that castle was garnished and furnished for a king and a queen royal there to have sojourned. And Sir Launcelot charged all his people to honour them and love them as they would do himself.

That about ends the story of Tristram and Isoud as far as Malory is concerned. True, there are several jousts, tourneys, and that sort of thing, but nothing germane to the love affair (no *Liebestod*). Presumably Blanche Mains waits uncheered, unkissed, and unclipped in Brittany, while King Mark sulks by himself in Cornwall.

I suppose somebody should rewrite *King Arthur and His Knights*. The revelations made so far are only a sample of what Sir James neglected to mention. Sir Gawain, for example, is nothing but a sixth-century version of Pal Joey, the perfect heel. When Sir Pelleas asks his friend Gawain to intercede for him with the lady Ettard, Gawain goes to bed with her instead—not that he loves her or has any thought of marrying her himself. In the same way, Lancelot refuses to legalize his affair with Elaine, in spite of the fact that she's about to become the mother of his son, the future Sir Galahad. As Lancelot takes pains to explain to another girl friend, also named Elaine: "I might have been married an I had would, but I never applied me yet to be married."

King Arthur's two half-sisters, Morgawse and Morgan le Fay, are more in the tradition. Morgawse is married to King Lot of Orkney and has four sons at the time she comes to visit her brother. Even incest takes on a rather casual tone as Malory describes it:

And thither came to him [Arthur] King Lot's wife, of Orkney, . . . and she came richly bisene, with her four sons Gawaine, Gaheris, Agravine, and Gareth, with many other knights and ladies. For she was a passing fair lady, therefore the king cast great love unto her, and desired to lie by her; so they were agreed, and he begat upon her Mordred, and she was his sister, on his mother's side, Igraine.

Arthur's other sister, Morgan le Fay, wife of King Uriens, makes out somewhat better despite her weakness for men. At any rate, she survives to attend her brother's funeral, which puts her one up on almost everyone else in the Arthurian legend. Her love life is a pattern for frustration. Her first lover, Sir Accolon, is killed by Arthur; her second, Sir Hemison, is liquidated by Sir Tristram. Sir Lancelot rejects her advances. Even more humiliating is her attempted seduction of a callow youth named Alisander, temporarily her prisoner. In Malory's account, she sends one of her young female relatives down to the dungeon with a message:

Sir, she said, wit you well that ye be a prisoner, and worse than ye ween; for my lady, my cousin Queen Morgan le Fay, keepeth you here for none other intent but for to do her pleasure with you when it liketh her. O Jesu defend me, said Alisander, from such pleasure; for I had lever cut away my hangers than I would do her such pleasure.

So the young cousin lets Alisander escape. Sir James would have us believe that Morgan le Fay is all pure villainy, but after reading Sir Thomas *and* Freud we can afford to feel sorry for her. But of all Sir James's sins of omission, the worst, in my opinion, was leaving out Sir Dinas and his dogs. Malory teaches a valuable lesson in common sense:

Now leave we off this tale, and speak we here of Sir Dinas that had within the castle a paramour, and she loved another knight better than him. And so when Sir Dinas went out on hunting she slipped down by a towel, and took with her two brachets. . . . And when Sir Dinas come home and missed his paramour and his brachets, then was he the more wrother for his brachets than for the lady. So then he rode after the knight that had his paramour, and bad him turn and joust. So Sir Dinas smote him down, that with the fall he brake his leg and his arm. And then his lady and paramour cried Sir Dinas' mercy, and said she would love him better than ever she did. Nay, said Sir Dinas, I shall never trust them that once betrayed me, and therefore as ye have begun so end, for I will never meddle with you. And so Sir Dinas departed, and took his brachets with him. . . .

And so we take our leave of both Sir James Knowles, K.C.V.O., and Sir Thomas Malory. Tennyson, anyone?

A full-time doctor (in Bridgeport, Conn.) and a part-time author (at home in nearby Fairfield), Kenneth R. Morgan is currently working on a novel which is not about medicine.

ME AND hIM WAS friends

BETTER ENGLISH FOR THE 1960'S?

In the February, 1960, issue of College English, *a monthly journal published by the National Council of Teachers of English, there appeared an article entitled "English Grammar in the 1960's" by Professor Ralph B. Long. The author, who taught for twenty-eight years at the University of Texas, now heads the English program of the University of Puerto Rico. In order to bring to the attention of parents and other interested readers an example of current thinking in certain educational circles,* HORIZON *reprints, with the Council's permission, two salient passages from Professor Long's paper:*

The grammar of the 1960's should be entirely analytic and systematic in organization and presentation. The structure of standard American English should be described simply, bit by bit, beginning in the early grades. When it is taught to children whose spoken English is nonstandard, it should be taught without any hint of righteousness. There should be no frontal attacks on the speech of homes and communities. Writing is a deliberate activity in which the grammatical patternings shared with speech are followed more scrupulously. Correction of nonstandard English can be achieved through composition—and through reading—quietly and gradually as vocabulary is acquired, with grammar used as a lever and not as a bludgeon. In the teaching of grammar the focus should never be on errors that are made or that might be made. It is important too that the analysis taught should grant informal standard English full equality with general standard English and should assign formal standard English the minor place it deserves. The pathetic elegancies of school-ma'am English must be given up. For any but quite formal use, it is hardly possible to revive *whom* and the *shall* of simple prediction, or to replace *can* with *may* where permission is asked or given, or to drive *was* out of wishes and rejected conditions. Good English is flexible, not rigid; and it is informal in style much more often than it is formal. . . .

Such sentences as *me and him was friends* cannot be called standard; but **they** occur, their structure is clear, and they are in fact the kind of thing the language **has** long tended toward, as in the historical displacement of *ye* by *you* and of *rid* by *rode.*

A PASSION FOR IVORY

CONTINUED FROM PAGE 94

mother by the last Manchu emperor, P'u Yi. It was an ivory sculpture of an ordinary clam shell no more than life size, but within its half-opened shell was a complete scene of a Chinese summer pavilion set among trees and shrubs, with a garden sloping down to a pond. On the pond were five ducks wearing collars. A man in a big straw hat stood on the bank holding a string attached to each of the collars. I recall with what amazement I first saw, with the aid of a strong magnifying glass, that each of these strings had been carved in the twisted form of a rope and that all were separately gathered into the minuscule right hand of the man! The ducks were about one millimeter long. How the artist could have done such work, even aided by powerful glasses, is really incomprehensible.

Allegedly there were once enormous ivory statues—or, rather, statues covered with ivory—in inner China and in India during early times, but it was apparently the Greeks who perfected this large-scale art. Ivory was known and used at the time of Homer in 800 B.C., but it came into its glory at the hands of the great artists of the classical period. Even though its application seems gaudy to us, ivory was not beneath the dignity of some of Greece's greatest sculptors. Theirs was a technique known as *chryselephantine*, in which ivory was combined with solid gold, cedar and other woods, gems and other precious substances. With these materials the Greeks made statues up to forty feet in height, like that of Minerva in the Parthenon. According to Pausanias such colossi were numerous; he mentions a Venus at Megara constructed by Praxiteles, a Hebe by Naucydes, and a vast work in gold and ivory by Phidias at Elis. The Romans later learned the art and erected hundreds of such effigies.

It seems that the Greeks learned from someone how to soften ivory. The Jews had long before made much use of it for thrones, couches, beds, and other furnishings, many of which were paneled with solid sheets of ivory; the Phoenicians even covered with ivory the seats of the rowers in their galleys. Wherever the softening method originated, the Greeks perfected it. Unfortunately, they have not left us any technical details, but there is a fifteenth-century recipe in a manuscript in the British Museum. It says that muriatic acid renders ivory as soft and pliable as wax; then it can be molded, and afterward it can be hardened again in white vinegar. It is believed that the ancients somehow softened the whole tusk; then they straightened it out and cut it in half longitudinally, obtaining "planks" up to two feet wide, or slit it down the top and flattened the whole out, getting planks up to four feet in width. It is also possible that they either prepared wood molds or, alternatively, had the whole statue already completed in hardwood. All those parts representing exposed skin would be covered by sheets of pliable ivory, which were then hardened with some adhesive beneath. "Clothing" was covered with gold sheet or leaf, while the thrones, base, and other appurtenances were left bare.

Ivory can be both dyed and etched. It is known that the Greeks and Romans colored their statuary, and ivory was apparently tinted to produce perfectly natural skin tones (ivory will take a very fine polish with chalk and wet leather, and it can be made to resemble the grain of flesh with rouge, a sponge, and sand). The eyes were painted in, and eyebrows, mustaches, and beards of real hair were added. The jewels were real gems, fingernails were made of polished cowhorn, scepters of bronze, and sandals of leather. It is little

FLORA'S FAUNA RISE IN REVOLT

How does a Latin-American revolution seem to an observer in innermost Tirol? The imaginative Innsbruck satirist Paul Flora interprets (with captions in his own tongue) the course of a faraway uprising, from proclamation through march on the capital, surrender of government troops, assassination of the president and looting of the national bank to a New Order.

PROKLAMIERUNG DER REVOLUTION DURCH GENERAL PORFIRIO NAVARRO

wonder that the ancients were awed by the colossal statues of their gods, for they must have been utterly lifelike.

The Romans were basically gadgeteers. They absorbed the arts of others as sponges suck up water, and they got most of their initial culture from the Etruscans. The Etruscans seem to have worked ivory, although where they got it is a mystery—unless they killed off the last European mammoths or retrieved buried caches of tusks. Ivory was a symbol of power to them, and they transferred its significance to the Romans, who not only held the material in the highest esteem but eventually went slightly mad over it, even using it as currency. Roman magistrates sat on thrones of ivory; consuls had chryselephantine chairs made in Etruria. They used ivory for dagger and sword hilts and on the harnesses of their steeds. Their "Congressional Record" was traditionally inscribed on ivory, as were the births, marriages, and deaths of their prominent citizens and their key census totals. They dyed it, encrusted it, etched it, and carved it. They made the first diptychs of it.

Diptychs were the standard stenographers' pads of the day: two slabs of ivory joined together by cord hinges, the inner faces of the slabs being slightly guttered and filled with a thin layer of wax. On these, Roman secretaries scratched notes with a stylus; the notes were preserved when the two leaves were closed. The outside of the leaves was carved with the name of the owner and with various designs and scenes. It became the practice for a newly appointed consul to present a number of diptychs to his sponsors, to local senators, and to other prominent persons on the occasion of his elevation to office. A few have been preserved. Later, these diptychs were adopted by the princes and bishops of the Roman Catholic Church. Often the carved portrait of the Roman consul was merely given a tonsure, the name of a saint inscribed below, and the note pad was made ready for use in recording sermons, hymns, and incantations. Some of these, too, have been preserved. Later came triptychs, and carved ivory (spelled in Middle English *iverey, eivry, yvory, ivery,* and various other ways) caskets containing the relics of saints and apostles. Then came crooks, pastoral staves, crucifixes, and just about every other church appurtenance in the same substance. Even the *flabellum* devised in the East to waft flies off the sacrament was traditionally made of ivory in the West.

Although ivory disappeared in secular circles after the fall of Rome, it soon reappeared in the form of sets of chessmen and other objects which were sent to Western potentates by the caliphs. In fact, we have a more continuous record of ivories than we have of any other European art form, with the possible exception of manuscripts.

And this material has held its place in our esteem; its fame and appreciation have spread all over the world, so that today there are ivory collectors scattered from Australia to South America and Soviet Russia. Much additional evidence has come to light, such as the fact that the most precious gift possible in the Fiji Islands turns out to be a sperm whale's tooth. Probably most surprising of all is the disclosure that ivory was worked in prehistoric times in the Americas, notably by the North American Indian—but this is another story.

And finally, although modern ingenuity has devised all manner of new substances unknown to nature itself—many of which look like ivory, will do everything ivory does, and even lack all of its drawbacks—ivory's place in our culture has never been seriously threatened.

Ivan T. Sanderson has been collecting and studying animals ever since he was seventeen, and writing books about them ever since Animal Treasure *beguiled so many readers in 1935.*

CH AUF DIE HAUPTSTADT   DIE KAPITULATION DER REGIERUNGSTRUPPEN

OUR FACE TO THE WORLD

CONTINUED FROM PAGE 9

underlies our prosperity, the psychological wear and tear of a moral system based on "success," the overweening preoccupation with national "greatness"—these we increasingly look upon as neurotic symptoms; mild, perhaps, but nonetheless the outcome of an outdated ethic we are trying to outgrow. Why should we ask the Asians and the Africans, who have not yet fatally succumbed to the modern virus, to live through the worst of the nineteenth century merely to arrive at a stage we are trying to leave? We have come through, and out the other side. Our abundance is de-puritanizing us, softening our harshness, making us more aware of one another, more concerned with private experience and the arts, more—in a word—Oriental. In a sense, we are asking the rest of the world to become sick at the very moment we show signs of becoming healthy.

Anyhow, assuming we had the capability, what are we trying to convey? To the extent that they have tasted imperial power, Americans have been chastened by it. After the war we discovered all too quickly that we could not lift our ways of doing things out of context and set them down anywhere with the same happy results. The more we tried to "sell" America, the more reluctant we became to engage in that unedifying activity. The more a Foreign Service officer has grappled with these prickly questions, the more likely he is to sympathize with Messrs. Kennan and Lippmann—and to urge that we deal with other people on a strict basis of what they want and what we want, and forget all that nonsense about the American example to mankind.

All of which I cannot help thinking would be a great loss, even if it were possible, which fortunately it isn't. The peoples of the impoverished continents have caught the smell of the twentieth century; they have the savor of it in their mouths, and they do not intend to go hungry. One way or another, they are going to pull themselves up into industrialism, and the question is not so much whether they will emulate us as it is what kind of "America" they are going to emulate. We no longer have the choice. We are the example, as we have been for many years. We have already been teaching, whether we wanted to or not, and sometimes to better effect than we knew.

For instance, between 1944 and 1946 we not only destroyed German and Japanese cities, we destroyed societies. One of them was the culture of the Manus, a people who live in the Admiralty Islands, north of New Guinea. There are some thirteen or fourteen thousand Manus, but in two years of war they were literally overrun by Americans—Americans of all shapes and sizes, of all possible states of grace, the statistical average of the United States Army. More than a million soldiers were staged through the Admiralties. We knocked the tops off hills, we dug new channels through the lagoons, we cut away the bush for airstrips and mile on mile of barracks. And everywhere were the Manus—watching, fascinated, the damnedest thing that had ever happened to them.

They got into everything: movies, engine rooms, chow lines—it was easier to hand them a tin tray than set up special facilities to feed them. They had known before about machines and the white man's way, but now they were thrown quite by accident into the very midst of it, and for the first time they could see how it operated. Previously they had lived in what can only be called the Stone Age, a cultural climate of economic stringency and ferocious taboo that Dr. Margaret Mead described in her book *Growing Up in New Guinea* (1930). Although their own culture was also of a piece, and worked for them, the Americans confronted them with a set of shattering experiences. They now refer to the years we were there as "the time without taboos," and after we left they decided to do an extraordinary thing.

FLORA'S FAUNA (CONTINUED)

DIE ERMORDUNG DES PRÄSIDENTEN OSCAR OROSCO

DIE AUSPLÜNDERUNG DER STAATSBANK

Aldous Huxley has spoken of armies as almost perfect non-conductors of culture, but in this event he was proved wrong. In the years between 1946 and 1950 the Manus simply scrapped their old society and set about building a new one, complete from top to bottom.

In 1953 Margaret Mead went back to the Admiralties to see what had happened to the Manus. She met many of the men and women she had known as children, and they told her about the Americans. The Manus were accustomed to being jealous and embittered over their few belongings, but the Americans "had so many possessions they did not have to quarrel and care about particular ones." The Manus love machinery, but they had not known before that it could be used to replace labor. "The Americans believe in having work done by machines," they told Miss Mead, "so that men can live to an old age instead of dying worn out while they are still young." A Manus named Raphael Manuwai told her, as she reports in her more recent book, *New Worlds for Old:* "From the Americans we learned that human beings are irreplaceable and unexpendable, while all material things are replaceable and so expendable. . . . From the Americans we learned that it is *only* human beings that are important."

All this the Manus learned from that bumbling, improvised, perennially discontented, and totally characteristic institution, the American Army. And so they went to work building what they call "the New Way"—new villages, new customs, new kinds of authority, new relationships between the sexes, new ideas of good and evil, and new and unforeseen difficulties. They have had to discover it all for themselves: how to run village meetings, how to draw lines between freedom and license, how to bring up children to be at home in this world as their parents were in the one that has now gone forever.

Therefore let us be of good heart. We can no more turn time back than the Manus can, nor can we become the people of such simple and coherent purposes that they imagine us to be. While their postwar revolution was in progress, the Manus underwent a "cargo cult," an outburst of the extravagant religious enthusiasm that has periodically affected many islands in the Pacific during the past century. Knowing of the white man's goods ("cargo") only that it came in ships, they conceived the idea that more ships were coming, filled with the same unimaginable riches that had come before, but this time sailed by black people and intended for them. The Manus now refer to their "cargo cult" somewhat ashamedly as "the Noise," but not all the beliefs behind it have disappeared. When one of the Manus who had momentarily adhered to the cult was questioned by an anthropologist from Miss Mead's mission, he was asked how—since he had seen so much of the American equipment and understood it so well—he could possibly think it was created out of nothingness. The Manus objected. "You can't tell me," he said, "you can't tell me a B-17 bomber was made by human hands."

So it will be a long time before we have taught them *all* the secrets. How to be an industrial-democratic society in the twentieth century is something the Americans know more about than most, but we know also that we have just begun to learn. This country is still an experiment, and what the watchful world most needs to know is whether we can make it work. We cannot become unwise again at will, or escape the nervous afflictions of responsibility, or slough off its weariness. We can only pursue our own voyage of self-discovery to its unforseeable end and exhaust the possibilities that go with being this particular people, on this particular land, at this particular moment in time. So doing, we can only hope that those who come to us for wise counsel will find what they seek, and that we will see reflected in their eyes our better selves.

This is the fourth in a series of inquiries by Mr. Larrabee into America's social order today. The third, "The Imaginary Audience," appeared in the March, 1960, issue of HORIZON.

DIE VERHAFTUNG DES ALS DAME VERKLEIDETEN
INNENMINISTERS ARTURO ROBLES

PORFIRIO NAVARRO UND DIE ÜBRIGEN HÄUPTER DER REVOLUTION

THE RAMPANT FOX

CONTINUED FROM PAGE 101

marriage with a virtuous Catholic lady, Maria Fitzherbert. Having received an assurance from the Prince that the prevalent rumors concerning his marriage were altogether baseless, Fox stood up to inform his fellow members that the report was a "calumny, destitute of all foundation, impossible ever to have happened, and propagated with the sole view of depreciating the Prince's character in the estimation of the country." He did not then know that the persuasive Prince, who, as Byron later acknowledged, had "fascination in his very bow," was a neurotic weakling of the most unstable type. When Fox spoke, the Prince was already married, although the marriage was secret and entirely illegal. It was not the last time that the erratic heir to the throne would delude and disappoint the Whig party.

This was in 1787; during the summer of the year 1789, revolution rocked the French throne. In July the Bastille fell, and its fall reverberated across Europe, shaking other thrones, terrifying Conservative governments, and stirring Liberal thinkers to tumultuous applause. "How much the greatest event it is that has ever happened in the world! [wrote Fox to his devoted friend Richard Fitzpatrick] and how much the best!" adding that, "if this Revolution has the consequences I expect," besides transforming France, it would revolutionize the whole system of European politics. Liberals might hope to come into their own; in 1789, as in 1917, a new era of human enlightenment seemed to be on the point of opening. But as the French Revolution developed, and high-minded theorists reappeared under the guise of ardent revolutionary terrorists, eighteenth-century Whigs were faced with the same dilemma that confronted twentieth-century men of good will when the Russian Revolution began to reveal its more appalling aspects.

Like them, Fox longed to believe in the rightness of the movement he had warmly welcomed—not only because even the bravest men are always reluctant to admit their errors, but because in the spirit of the Revolution, though not in its political effects, he felt that he had recognized an enduring force for good. In the meantime, a new adversary had arisen to dominate the House of Commons. Pitt was an opponent Fox could not despise, as he had once despised the hapless Lord North: still young, yet strangely majestic, cold, zealous, without personal failings (though there were occasions when he reached the House extremely drunk), impassive and incorruptible, an unflinching martyr to his sense of duty. In his earliest days he had advocated Reform and recommended that parliamentary representation should be reorganized on broader, less oligarchic lines. But revolution abroad and the threat of revolution at home drove Pitt into the opposite camp; and as a war minister he retaliated with draconian edicts against any suspicion of subversive activity.

The witch hunt that his government conducted was car-ried to ridiculous and fantastic lengths. And while a war fever swept through Great Britain, Fox and his Whig allies undertook the difficult and unpopular task of explaining and excusing events abroad insofar as that was still possible— Marie Antoinette's trial and execution, Fox agreed, had been "attended with every circumstance that could contribute to make the act more disgusting and detestable than any other murder recorded in history"—and at home opposing the reactionary measures constantly introduced by Pitt's cabinet. "Prosecutions intolerable [he noted], both here and in Scotland are going on every day, and nobody seems to mind them. The very name of Liberty is scarce popular." Such prosecutions, he asserted, were at once oppressive and uncalled-for; he refused to believe that an English revolution might even then be getting under way: "An insurrection! Where is it? Where has it reared its head? Good God! an insurrection in Great Britain!" Two gentlemen had presumed to assure the House that a state of revolt had existed for the last fortnight, "but they have given us no light whatever, no clue, no information where to find it. . . . I will take it upon me to say, sir, that it is not the notoriety of the insurrections which prevents these gentlemen from communicating to us the particulars, but their non-existence."

Yet Fox's personal sympathies were still sharply divided; and although he deprecated alarmist measures and ridiculed the revolutionary scare, his own conduct at this period was sometimes calculated to increase the general confusion. Had he not, when asked to propose a loyal toast at a public dinner organized by the Duke of Norfolk, suggested that the company should raise their glasses to "our Sovereign's health —the Majesty of the People"? There was a moment, indeed, when he seemed to be becoming the *enfant terrible* of his own party; his controversial utterances dismayed the Whigs almost as much as they disturbed the government. Pitt thought that the idea of committing Fox to the Tower of London certainly "deserved consideration"; Burke, the archopponent of Gallic revolutionary principles, had already broken with him after many years of friendship—"Mr. Burke [Fox later announced] deemed the sacrifice necessary," though it had cost him "the most heartfelt pain"; and conservative caricaturists began to portray Fox either as a double-faced monster, part Jacobin, part English gentleman, or as a sadistic sans-culotte, scourging a half-naked Pitt bound to a whipping-post erected in the middle of St. James's Street, while bishops were butchered on the balcony of Brooks's, White's Club went up in flames, and London's pavements streamed with blood.

On the other hand, his strong good sense never quite deserted him; and as the revolutionary wars ran their costly, inconclusive course, he was perpetually campaigning for a negotiated settlement. That Great Britain must be defended, he could not deny; but national defense, he insisted, might easily be confused with a policy of international aggression. "Any plan of aggrandizement founded on the present distressed situation in France, much less any purpose of establishing among the French people any particular form of government," was plainly undeserving of his countrymen's support. But, as an advocate of peace, he spoke to little effect; and during the early summer of 1797, the Whig opposition, with Fox at their head, decided to withdraw from the House of Commons, announcing, as a dramatic gesture of protest, that they would take no further part in parliamentary proceedings. Fox himself retired to St. Ann's Hill, there to enjoy his gardens and fields and the serene society of his beloved Elizabeth; while his bold young lieutenant, Charles Grey, who thirty-five years later was to become the architect of the First Reform Bill, retreated to his estates in Northumberland and the arms of a newly married wife.

Apart from a visit to Paris during the short-lived Peace of Amiens, Fox remained almost uninterruptedly at St. Ann's Hill from 1797 to 1806; and, despite his anguished preoccupation with the state of war-torn Europe, it would appear to have been one of the happiest periods of his whole existence. A small bow-fronted house on the crest of a gentle slope, his place of retirement satisfied every need. He could entertain his friends from London with music, wine, and conversation; walk at his leisure along the Surrey lanes, pausing now and then to lean over a gate and discuss the prospects of the hay crop; read and discuss his favorite poets, English, Latin, Greek, Italian; or lie for hours on a sunlit lawn pleasantly resigned to doing nothing. Yet although he loved idleness, still he could not altogether disregard the urgent claims of public business; and in 1806, when Pitt died, bitterly "lamenting the misfortunes of his country"—the news of Napoleon's victory at Austerlitz had dealt him the final deadly blow—Fox for the last time returned to Westminster and for the last time accepted a high office.

As Foreign Secretary and Leader of the House of Commons in the so-called "Ministry of All the Talents," he displayed his usual diligence and energy and was able to frame and put through a measure that immensely lightened the burden of human suffering: the bill that he introduced on March 31 marked the first important step toward the abolition of the slave trade. His parliamentary career, he reminded the House, had now lasted for almost forty years; and if that bill had been his only achievement, "I should think that I had done enough, and could retire from public life with comfort, and conscious satisfaction, that I had done my duty." In fact he was not to retire until a physical breakdown forced his hand. At fifty-seven he was growing old, and that summer his health showed signs of failing. His nephew suggested that he should accept a peerage, but Fox brushed the ridiculous suggestion aside: "I have an oath in Heaven against it; I will not close my politics in that foolish way, as so many have done before me." Abolition and peace were "two such glorious things" that he could not, would not, give them up. Meanwhile symptoms of dropsy appeared,

and as the summer drew to a close, his friends recognized that his case was hopeless. He died on September 13, 1806, calm, uncomplaining, even humorous; and his last words were reserved for his incomparable wife, *sostegno della mia vita*. "I die happy," he said, "but I pity you." And then, as if he feared that his farewell had been a shade too solemn and pathetic: "It don't signify, my dearest, dearest Liz."

Any appraisal of Fox's character presents the modern historian with a somewhat difficult task. For the last hundred and fifty years, a host of critics have dwelt delightedly upon his private failings; and since they were failings he did not trouble to conceal, nineteenth-century moralists found him an easy victim. "He had three passions [we are told]—women, play, and politics. Yet he never formed a creditable connexion with a woman; he squandered all his means at the gaming table, and except for eleven months he was invariably in opposition." This diatribe, it is clear, includes several odd inaccuracies: his connection with Elizabeth Armistead was greatly to the credit of both partners, and during the space that he held office—for eighteen, not eleven months—he accomplished as much as a good many statesmen have managed to cram into a whole decade. But even Fox's more sensible contemporaries agreed that his character had some serious flaws. Philip Francis alleged that "he had no heart"—was Francis, though, a very good judge?—and it is generally admitted that in questions of money he was apt to be selfish and unscrupulous, rarely averse from borrowing though often reluctant to discharge his debts.

Yet when all is said, how many virtues remain, and how endearing is the personal impression he leaves! His father's spoiling had implanted bad habits, but had failed to damage his essential qualities; and few happier or less unbalanced men have ever embarked upon a public career. He had nothing of the grim self-absorption that disfigures the average statesman's portrait; for Fox was primarily a man of the world, in the broadest and most civilized meaning of the term: a lover of poetry who worshiped Homer and Shakespeare and had made a close study of the works of Chaucer, a great traveler, an admirable boon companion, a student of life who, when he spoke to his fellow human beings—scholars, jockeys, farmers, fashionable women—always used their own language. Whether he worked or idled, he did so with consummate zest, for he had learned the art of becoming entirely absorbed in every occupation that took his fancy. Charles James Fox gardened and farmed as enthusiastically as Churchill paints, and he discovered unending "sources of enjoyment" in a variety of far more trivial pastimes. Thus, after an arduous spell of politics, we hear that he drove down to Cheltenham and, on his holiday, spent much of the leisure he had earned trying patiently to tame a young rabbit.

Peter Quennell is co-editor of the English magazine History Today. *An excerpt from his most recent book,* The Sign of the Fish, *appeared in the January, 1960, issue of* HORIZON.

By GILBERT HIGHET

THEIR NAMES AR[E]

Poor Saint Audrey is buried in a

garden and Lord Sandwich's nam[e]

There are many kinds of fame, some to be desired, some, perhaps, to be avoided. One of the strangest is that which preserves the name of a man alone, while the man himself is entirely forgotten. There is another, almost equally bizarre, by which the man's name survives as a word used by millions of people, while the man is remembered quite apart from the word which was once, as it were, part of him. In most Western languages the seventh month of the year is called July and the eighth month of the year is called August (or some close variants of these names); and most people in the Western world have heard of Julius Caesar and his successor, the Emperor Augustus, but do we ever remember that July was called after Julius and August after Augustus? Occasionally the name is well known, while we recall only a fragment of the man's own history. That is one way in which myths are born. For example, was there ever a real Judge Lynch who administered his own Lynch law? Some authorities give him a local habitation and a full name. They

say he was Charles Lynch, a Virginia planter and justice of the peace, and in the troubled times of the American War of Independence, he and other Whigs used to arrest "Tories and desperadoes," try them without any of the law's delays, and order immediate punishment. (You will be surprised, as I was, to learn that the punishment was usually flogging.) This all sounds real enough, yet there are those who believe that the name Lynch should be traced to other times and other countries, as the practice itself most certainly can.

When we can discover the man behind the name, his life history is often surprising. One of the most famous of these name owners was an apparently insignificant and conventional Englishman who died about sixty years ago. Call him X. He was the son of a clergyman in Norfolk, served for some time as an officer in the British army, retired, and took a job as agent for a wealthy landowner. The landowner was having serious trouble with his tenants, who demanded an across-the-board reduction in rents, first 10 per cent and later 25 per cent. He refused to make the concessions. The tenants refused to pay rent. Now it was the job of Mr. X to make them pay or get out. He procured notices of eviction and sent court officials, accompanied by police, to serve them; but it was useless. An angry crowd gathered and drove both police and process servers away. The tenant farmers had a powerful union, and its leader advised them, if they were refused a reduction in rent, "to take certain measures against the landlords and their representatives." It was X who first felt the full brunt of these "measures." He had a farm of his own but he could get no one to work on it. His walls were broken down. His cattle were stampeded to fret them and make them thin. He could not even buy food, and had to order everything he needed from many miles away. When he left his house he was yelled at and spat upon. The climax came in November, 1880, when his crops were in danger of rotting in the fields. Fifty volunteers from outside came in to harvest them, and they were protected by a force of nine hundred soldiers with two field guns. (History does not record where he sold his produce, or what he

WRIT IN WEBSTER

adjective, but Bégon blooms in the

is literally on everyone's tongue

got for it.) He was Captain Charles Cunningham Boycott, the agent for Lord Erne in County Mayo from 1873 to 1886. Ever since his painful adventures, anyone who has been shunned and ignored and treated as an outcast has been said to suffer a boycott.

The curious thing about the case of Captain Boycott is that in the end it was less serious than it appeared. In 1880 and 1881, when the Irish Land League agitation was at its hottest, he must often have wondered whether he would ever live to see his fiftieth birthday. Indeed he often looked death in the face. He got letters with threats of murder in them; he was mobbed when he attended a country auction; and—in a ceremony which looks either silly or sinister, depending on where you stand—he was hanged in effigy, and his effigy was burned to ashes. But in 1881 the Land League was dissolved, and things returned to normal. Captain Boycott carried on as before; he lived down his unpopularity; and later, when he became a land agent in the southeast of England, he even used to go to Ireland for his vacations. He need not have been very intelligent, Captain Boycott, and surely most Irishmen would say he was the instrument of an evil policy, but there is no doubt of one thing: he had courage.

Many men who were once far more eminent and proud than Captain Charles Cunningham Boycott are now wholly forgotten except by specialists. Their names alone live on. Even the names would sometimes be unrecognizable to the dignitaries who once bore them. Consider the Lord of Villemain, whose name was Jean Nicot. In his time he was both noble and distinguished, for his king sent him to be the ambassador of France at the court of Portugal. But in the Encyclopædia Britannica there is no entry under his name; his diplomatic achievements (whatever they were) are forgotten. Only his name lives, because on his way home he brought back to Paris a strange new herb imported from the lately discovered American continent, and in his honor the plant was named Nicotiana and the essence of the plant nicotine. Or consider Michel Bégon, who administered the French West Indies for the great King Louis XIV. An ad-

ILLUSTRATIONS BY WALTER EINSEL

mirable official, generous and wise, a patron of science, a discriminating collector of rarities, he is now recalled only because a botanist to whom he had shown kindness named the begonia after him. His contemporary Pierre Magnol was a quiet professor who worked in Montpellier and earned the gratitude of *some* gardeners by arranging the plants into families. No doubt Donald Culross Peattie knows him well; you and I hear only an echo of his surname in that charming group of shrubs and trees called magnolia.

Could you wish for a sweeter sort of immortality? If anyone deserves remembrance, surely we should remember the saints with affection and admiration. Yet poor Saint Etheldreda has not inherited such a memory. She was a Saxon lady, and apparently she was beautiful, for she loved dressing up and wearing fine jewelry. But she became more and more withdrawn from the world and devoted to religion. When she was dying, she said that the tumor on her neck was God's punishment for her love of necklaces. She was

127

honored. Every year in the town of Ely they held a fair to commemorate her virtues, and sold cheap necklaces of wood and bone, together with lace neckpieces and trimmings. As time went on, her name, Etheldreda, was smoothed out into Audrey, and the easily tarnished lace sold at the fair of Saint Audrey was called tawdry lace; so now any cheap frippery is known to us as tawdry.

The Russians are very fond of calling us hooligans and chauvinists. The first hooligan was a tough Irish immigrant to England who lived with his family in south London. He was strong, and his neighbors thought he was unduly addicted to bashing people, and now the name of Patrick Houlihan, or Hooligan, has become a byword. As for poor Nicolas Chauvin, he was a veteran of Napoleon's Grand Army, wounded seventeen times, who never ceased to proclaim his loyalty to his emperor, so much that he had the misfortune to make himself absurd. At last he became a character in a French musical show whose author ridiculed extravagant displays of patriotism in the song *"Je suis français, je suis Chauvin!"* And now chauvinism is any kind of patriotism of which someone else disapproves; the Russians do not call their war against Germany the Great Chauvinist Conflict, but the Great Patriotic War.

Poor Sergeant Chauvin! Poor Saint Audrey! Yet even the fate which befell these name bearers is not so fantastic as the destiny of two English noblemen whose names are immortalized by their own little domestic inventions: one of them known and recalled by name ten thousand times a day in Britain and, although perhaps not quite so often in the United States, still far from being unfamiliar here; the other's title spread over nearly every menu from San Francisco to Vienna, multiplied by dozens of inventive variations, and popular in a small way with everyone from the age of seven to the age of seventy. These noblemen were, first, the Earl of Cardigan, and, second, the Earl of Sandwich. It is difficult to appreciate and admire the proud, pompous, selfish, magnificent European aristocrats, unless (like the Esterházys of Hungary) they harbor a good composer or (like the Estes of Ferrara) encourage the drama and the visual arts. But these two noble earls, though fabulously rich and powerful, were admired by practically no human being except themselves and their toadies. One of them was a handsome, arrogant ass. The other was a shambling, treacherous scoundrel. What is particularly comic is the fact that the sandwich, which we all think of as being a nice, simple, unpretentious food, was invented by (or for) the Earl of Sandwich, who habitually led a life as luxurious as he could possibly manage to achieve on his own huge income and the money he got out of the British taxpayer. Similarly, the cardigan, the cozy woolen jacket which buttons up the front (and which, in Britain, is usually worn by those who like comfort and do not care whether they are dowdy or not), was invented by (or for) the superb James Thomas Brudenell, seventh Earl of Cardigan, an army officer whose favorite costume was a uniform of cherry-colored trousers, a royal blue jacket edged with gold, a furred pelisse, a short coat thrown over the shoulders and glittering with gold lace, and a high fur hat with brilliant plumes on it. The Earl is never known to have wept; but if he had seen the sad, mousy-brown, sagging, and often slightly smelly garment by which his name is now perpetuated, he would surely have given the performance which accompanied his habitual fits of anger, writhing his body, distorting his handsome features, and making the veins on his temples and forehead bulge with fury.

As for the Earl of Sandwich, there is no biography of him. Someone with an interest in satire and a thorough knowledge of the eighteenth century ought to write a life of John Montagu, who became the fourth Earl of Sandwich at the age of eleven and spent more than forty years in politics. During his career he helped to lose the American colonies (need I remark that he was an influential member of Lord North's Cabinet?) and very nearly wrecked the British navy by allowing a fantastic net of bribery and corruption to be spread all through it. (One of the chief British battleships, the *Royal George,* sank in still water at Spithead harbor because a large piece of her bottom fell out.) The only reason Sandwich ever left politics was that his kept mistress was murdered by an unsuccessful lover, and his peculiar family arrangements drew unpleasant publicity upon him. As for the simple and healthful sandwich, he invented that about the year 1762, when he spent twenty-four solid hours at the gambling table without taking any food except slices of cold roast beef between slices of toast.

The other, that monumental ass, the seventh Earl of Cardigan, has been admirably described, with a pen dipped in clear acid, by Mrs. Cecil Woodham-Smith in one of the most intelligent books of historical reconstruction I have ever read: *The Reason Why* (published by McGraw-Hill). It was Cardigan who led the famous Charge of the Light Brigade. He led it because he was extremely brave and extremely stupid and because he was in the middle of a violent feud with several other noblemen who held military commands in the same army. He failed to do anything with it, apparently because he could not think what to do when the charge reached its objective, the Russian guns; he simply rode back again, without his men, whom he left to find their own way home through shot and shell. And the only reason he invented the cardigan was that—although during the campaign he lived on his yacht in Balaclava harbor—he found the Russian climate rather chilly.

But here is one of the most striking oddities about names transformed into words. Suppose the Earl of Cardigan had been an ardent gambler, and suppose the Earl of Sandwich had been a keen cavalryman who fought in the Crimean War. In that case, on a cold winter day, you might find yourself wearing a sandwich and eating a cardigan.

THROUGH THE AGES
IN THE BEST BEDS

Solace and civilization have been combined in them

Primeval man really got off the ground when he devised a better way of sleeping than on the bare earth. Great ages thereafter produced great beds, and the more uses to which a bed was put, besides slumber, the higher the civilization. Ancient Egypt and Mesopotamia made the bed also a place for feasting—a custom next adopted by the Greeks and Romans in their time of glory. In feudal England, an invitation to share the bed of a noble and his family was reputedly an honor, and the expansive Elizabethan age culminated in the Great Bed of Ware (see page 130), which could sleep twenty-four. French kings up to the Revolution dispensed justice from their beds, and in the reign of Louis XIV the bed became a veritable cult, the monarch and titled ladies all receiving callers while reclining. This was the golden age of France and of the bed. America's own history of bedmanship ranges from the "bundling" of Puritan courting couples to the contemporary "think" bed for busy executives, complete with built-in magazine rack, chessboard, and Dictaphone —and back to the rudimentary pad of the beatnik.

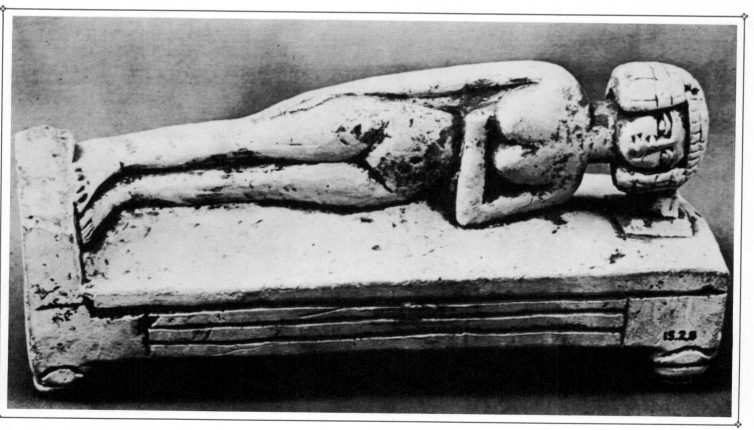

This wooden bed with headrest offered small comfort to an Egyptian lady of the 18th Dynasty

Built by neolithic dwellers of Skara Brae in the Orkneys, this bed consisted of stone slabs laid on the ground near their hearth.

King Ashurbanipal conformed to Assyrian custom by dining alone in his bed, while his wife sat apart.

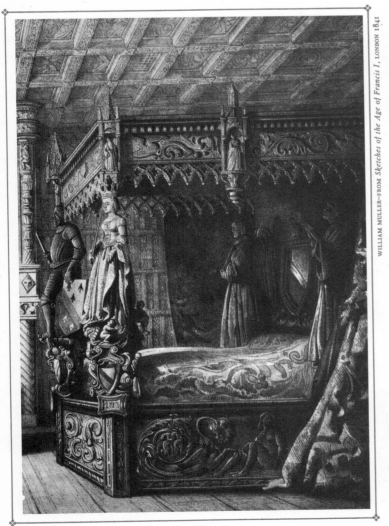

The carpenter's art soared in these medieval bedposts of lords, ladies, and praying angels, in the Loire château of Azay-le-Rideau.

The Dutch used a stepladder to climb into their bed cabinet, decorated with fine delftware. Two doors shut out drafts—and air.

ROBERT VON SPALART—FROM *Tableau Historique des Costumes* . . . . PARIS 1804

A Norman bed, its head higher than its foot, raised the occupant to nearly sitting position for greater agility in case of enemy attack.

A pile of soft rugs often formed the well-inhabited Persian bed, surmounted by a sloping canopy if outdoors.

VICTORIA AND ALBERT MUSEUM

So famous was the size of the Bed of Ware, that Shakespeare mentioned it in *Twelfth Night*

Upward and on with man's essential home furnishing

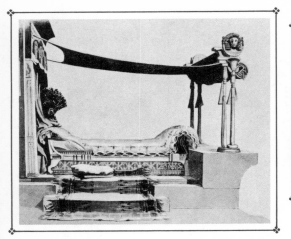

Cleopatra might have relaxed on such an Egyptian couch topped with canopy.

Pompeian beds were narrow and served as much for lounging and taking meals as for sleeping.

Medieval beds in cold baronial halls often required massive draperies.

The French Renaissance added gay carvings to an oak frame.

Italy, at the same time, added a tapestry-covered wardrobe closet.

These posts and valances framed the bed of Queen Victoria's mother.

Before the deluge overtook her, Marie Antoinette slept here.

Louis XV's state bed, built like a stage, displayed lavish fabrics.

In her *lit de repos,* a lady of fashion received friends and gossiped away the hours.

Unexpected guests were welcome in the eudal "Trinity," or three beds in one.

Built in a movable frame, the Breton bed formed part of the living room furniture.

Many a feather quilt was piled upon this Scandinavian sleeping place of wood and metal.

enice in its prime took to wrought n and old silk damask hangings.

Members of the Japanese imperial family favored this slender teak frame.

The canopy of this Russian oak bed was hung from chains on crossbars.

The cozy American colonial four-poster, a favorite in its time, remains a decorator's choice to this day.

The state bed of George IV, topped by a crown, was a fine Hepplewhite.

Despite the baldachin, the First Empire sought the look of ancient Greece and Rome.

The Illustrated London News 1858

Modern Europe, BY CHARLES HAZEN, HOLT, NEW YORK 1917

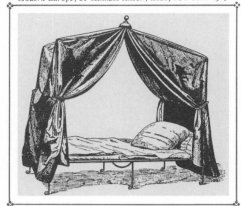

Napoleon's simple camp bed (above) was a mobile cot heavily curtained for privacy.

This Tudor cradle (left), crested and plumed, once harbored Queen Elizabeth I.

KOLLAR—CHRISTOFLE, PARIS

WALTER CARONE—*Paris Match*

The fertile imagination of an Indian rajah in Paris created the custom-made silver bed above, flanked by four bedposts in the form of nudes. His weight on the bed set off a music box and caused the women's arms to wave fans and fly whisks.

The French master Henri Matisse (left), though partially bedridden in his 80's, could sketch portraits on his bedroom wall using charcoal attached to a stick. Other men who created famous works in bed were Mark Twain and Marcel Proust.

Where fame and fantasy found their rest

Sarah Bernhardt, toast of two continents, sought her moments of solitude on the pelt-covered bed of her eccentric studio in Paris's Boulevard Pereire. A visiting reporter found her there "lounging, curving, on a divan, lost amid the brocades and furs," which included skins of bear, beaver, tiger, moose, and jaguar. The silk canopy above her was braided with dying flowers.